PRAISE FOR *Up Until Now*

"Infused with heartbreak, hurt, and hope, this brilliant and inspiring collection of short stories is sure to give you clarity in the face of fear, to be passionately, and outrageously devoted to living life. Not just any life, a life you absolutely love. I held this profound and courageous book about traversing adversity and transforming the condition into abundance, to my heart. I am confident you will as well."

—Mary Morrissey, International Speaker, Best-Selling Author, Founder of Brave Thinking Institute™

"WOW! This book truly captures the power of the human spirit. The stories in this book demonstrate the multitudes of heartache, fear and brokenness that people deal with daily. But more than that, it's how these amazing people overcome these problems and turn them into something beautiful that will grab your heart and leave you transformed. Once you pick up this book, you won't be able to put it down."

—Mathew Boggs, Best-Selling Author & Co-Founder Brave Thinking Institute™

"Knowledge comes from what one has learned, while wisdom is obtained from what one has lived. Laura brings both!"

—Logan Stout, Best-Selling Author, Speaker, Entrepreneur

"Be inspired and enriched reading Laura's incredible lessons of self-transformation. Up Until Now reveals in warm, purpose-filled stories the seeds of wisdom embodied within life's obstacles and challenges, as Laura reminds us to live our best life!"

—Ryan Stubbs, Author, Executive Coach, Former Knowledge Officer at the world's largest oil company.

"Laura has done a beautiful job showcasing a collection of short stories filled with insight, wisdom, and authenticity. Life lessons of hope, fear, clarity and transformation will leap out at you with the turning of each page, leaving you asking yourself one very important question, Am I living a life that I love?"

—Wendy Ditta, International Best Selling Author of "The More I Learn, The More I love."

"These Authors are delightful and inspiring to read. On more than one occasion I fought back tears. These stories pack serious punch and emotion as many of them are relatable and inspirational."

—Mark Moseley, NFL MVP 1982, Washington Commanders

"This book is a must-read! It includes an inspiring story for everyone and left me deeply inspired, motivated, and excited about living the life I have always dreamed of."

—Kortnye Hurst, International Model

"Up Until Now" is a true masterpiece! Threading heart-felt stories from heart-led leaders throughout this collection, Laura weaves together a shining tapestry of both transformation and triumph that will uplift, encourage and inspire you like no other. Each story makes its own unique impact on the reader and delivers actionable ways to overcome obstacles, push past fear, and achieve real life change!"

—Jennifer Maret Moran, SUCCESS 125 Finalist, Founder & CEO of GrowWithJMo Coaching, Maxwell Leadership Certified Coach/Trainer/Speaker, 2x Bestselling Author of "Purpose, Passion & Profit" and "Success Habits of Super Achievers"

# UP UNTIL NOW

INSPIRED STORIES FROM
REAL PEOPLE ON HOW TO
**EMBRACE YOUR FEAR
MOVE FORWARD AND
TRANSFORM YOUR LIFE**

## LAURA K WALKER

Up Until Now

Copyright © 2022

All rights reserved. All content is subject to copyright and may not be reproduced in any form without express written consent from the author. Although the author and publisher have made every effort to ensure that the information in this book was correct at press time, the author and publisher do not assume and hereby disclaim any liability to any party for any loss, damage, or disruption caused by errors or omissions, whether such errors or omissions result from negligence, accident, or any other cause.

Published by Elevate Publishing

ISBN 979-8-9862830-2-9 (paperback)
ISBN 979-8-9862830-6-7 (hardcover)

Printed in the United States of America

The inspiration that lies within these pages is dedicated to *Knowing*.

Knowing you are created for more—for greatness! It's that knowing part of you that faces fear and embraces Faith, regardless of the hurt or terror that keeps you stifled or stuck; unfulfilled.

Deep gratitude and appreciation go out to each precious soul that added their vulnerable, real story to this book for the sole purpose of inspiring and encouraging those that will read the amazing content and curriculum held inside.

May you be blessed beyond measure. Gratitude abounds for each of you.

There are no words to express my appreciation to Hanson Morris for the inspirational insight of this publication. You are a gift!

# Contents

| | |
|---|---|
| INTRODUCTION | 1 |
| LINDA WALKER \| *The Gift* | 7 |
| LORALEE BROER \| *Needle in a Haystack* | 9 |
| JUDY COOPER \| *Inner Critic* | 13 |
| STEVE DOTSON, DC \| *The Seeds of My Becoming* | 17 |
| KIRSTEN FAGAN \| *Life is a Gift* | 23 |
| DAWN L. HARGRAVES, ESQ. \| *FFMG* | 27 |
| DIANA CHERRYN KELLY, PHD \| *This World to the Next: Who Says They Don't Live On?* | 31 |
| ELLEN MOSELEY-MAY \| *Setting Down the Weight* | 41 |
| APRIL MAZZONI \| *Oops, I did it, again! (breathe . . .)* | 45 |
| CYNTHIA MORALES \| *A New Legacy* | 51 |
| NIKKI GEORGE PAPADAKIS \| *The Courage to Decide* | 59 |
| JACK SMITH, JR. \| *The Art of Charity* | 63 |
| JANETTE WOLD \| *Peace Keeping* | 67 |
| MATT ALEXANDER \| *Making it Out of the Darkness* | 73 |
| DANI ATKINS \| *The Unlearning of Unhappiness* | 77 |
| MAUREEN CONNELLY \| *My Life as a Nurse* | 83 |
| SVETLANA FARWELL \| *The Angel's Hand* | 89 |

| | |
|---|---|
| SCOTT & TIFFANY FINKELSTEIN \| *The Best is Yet to Come* | 93 |
| HANNAH KERSEY \| *Onward and Upward* | 97 |
| PHILIP KERSEY \| *Finding Me* | 103 |
| TODD MILLER \| *In the Nick of Time* | 109 |
| SHANNON PATTILLO \| *Saying Yes to Me* | 117 |
| JAMIE SALERNO \| *Grateful* | 121 |
| JACKIE SCOTT \| *Why Stop Now?* | 125 |
| ABBIE HABERSKI \| *Feather From Heaven* | 129 |
| CYNTHIA A MCQUADE-BRINKMAN \| *Morning Prayers* | 133 |
| PATRICK BLAHA \| *Finding My Place In Life* | 137 |
| SHARON BRYANT \| *Time For Change* | 143 |
| JUDY COOPER \| *Courage* | 147 |
| KIRSTEN FAGAN \| *I Choose Joy* | 151 |
| LAUREN GIULIANI \| *From Fired to Teacher of the Year (Almost)* | 155 |
| RENEE HILL, PH.D. \| *From Poverty to Ph. D.* | 161 |
| TODD MILLER \| *A Reunion of Friendship* | 167 |
| ANAMARI PEREZ \| *The Seahorse Miracle* | 173 |
| CYNTHIA PORTER \| *Empty Nesting is Not Always Pretty* | 179 |
| WENDY REVELL \| *My Identity* | 183 |
| CRYSTAL SCHUDER \| *A Phone Nudge from Heaven* | 189 |
| JACKIE SCOTT \| *Cyrus's Spaghetti Lesson* | 193 |
| ANGIE SINN \| *Choices* | 199 |
| KEN STIVER, M.D. \| *Migraine, A Lesson to Remember* | 203 |
| RENEE TOWNSEND \| *Rising Above* | 209 |
| KEENAN WHITAKER \| *In the Blink of An Eye* | 217 |
| KIRSTEN FAGAN \| *Guardian Angels and Facing Fears* | 223 |

| | |
|---|---|
| JACKIE SCOTT \| *Friday's Coffee Revelation* | 227 |
| LAURA WALKER \| *From a Broken Heart to Love on the Eiffel Tower* | 233 |
| **FEATURED CONTRIBUTORS** | 243 |
|     MATT ALEXANDER | 245 |
|     DANI ATKINS | 247 |
|     LORALEE BROER | 248 |
|     MAUREEN CONNELLY | 249 |
|     JUDY COOPER | 250 |
|     STEVEN DOTSON, DC | 252 |
|     KIRSTEN FAGAN | 253 |
|     SVETLANA FARWELL | 254 |
|     SCOTT FINKELSTEIN | 255 |
|     TIFFANY MARTIN FINKELSTEIN | 256 |
|     DAWN L. HARGRAVES, ESQ. | 257 |
|     DIANA CHERRYN KELLY, PH.D. | 258 |
|     HANNAH KERSEY | 260 |
|     PHILIP KERSEY | 261 |
|     ELLEN MOSELEY-MAY | 262 |
|     APRIL MAZZONI | 264 |
|     TODD MILLER | 265 |
|     CYNTHIA MORALES | 267 |
|     NIKKI GEORGE PAPADAKIS | 268 |
|     SHANNON PATTILLO | 269 |
|     JAMIE SALERNO | 270 |
|     JACKIE SCOTT | 271 |
|     JACK SMITH JR. | 272 |
|     LINDA WALKER | 273 |
|     JANETTE WOLD | 274 |
| **ABOUT THE AUTHOR** | 275 |

# *Introduction*

*Up Until Now* . . . three magical words.

Too bad I wasn't aware of them and their power until my late forties! In 2016, I was weathering divorce number two (not the proudest moment of my life) and was facing my fifties. Sad, depressed, and scared to mention but a few of the emotions I was feeling, I found myself in a downward spiral. Looking back now, I am pretty sure I owe my four amazing kiddos an apology because it could not have been fun for them to watch or navigate through their mother having a daily meltdown as young adults . . . So, "kids, I'm sorry and I love you so much!"

The year 2016 rounded into 2017 and as the seasons evolved into fall without mercy, October arrived unceremoniously. My emotions matched the season: somber, gray, sad. Within the first few days of October 2017, a phone call came from what I would have called an acquaintance. I knew her, but we were not close friends. At least not the kind of gal pals that texted and met regularly for coffee or wine. She lived in Louisiana, and I lived in Texas, and we knew each other because we were involved in some business endeavors together, over the past few years. She called announcing that she was coming into town and was attending a personal development workshop. She invited me to attend.

Immediately my fear radar went up like a siren in my head!

*Workshop??!! Do I need fixing? Who told Wendy I needed fixing? Who's the one that ratted me out?! They are in BIG trouble!*

As we chatted on the phone, I invited Wendy to stay in my small garden home as a guest and the night she arrived, it was determined that I was going to the workshop with her the next morning.

I didn't really want to go. Let's be honest, I had the whole weekend free and had planned to sleep in, eat and be lazy, now it appeared that the weekend was going to be used up "fixing Laura." But she had invested $250 in my ticket plus a VIP lunch ticket with the speaker, so I obliged out of Southern courtesy.

The rest is history and as we say in my line of work, that was my perception, *Up Until Now* . . .

The weekend workshop in Dallas, TX was a wakeup call. A loud and clear wakeup call. I was making marginal to bad choices in most areas of my life and there seemed to be a pattern in me that continued to attract more of the same lousy results. In men, in my health, in my finances, in work, and in my relationships with family and friends.

I was ready for change! Real CHANGE! But *Up Until Now*, I didn't know *how* to change . . .

However, now, change had arrived in the form of a workshop to "fix Laura."

As my mindset shifted and my heart, soul, and knowing evolved, my life began to reflect promise, hope and a glimmer of happiness. True happiness, for the first time in years. Or maybe EVER. . . . I was finally figuring out who I was, as well as Who's I was and what that meant in my journey going forward. I had a new expanded Knowing.

As COVID-19 arrived in 2020, life changed for everyone. I owned two companies. One was a large window company that required crews to service residential and commercial windows across our metroplex. There was no work. Let me repeat, due to Covid there was no work in my industry; no one wanted my crews inside of their home. So even though I was enjoying the lockdown much like everyone else was, as if it was a lovely mini vacation, panic began to set in. Worry, dread, and fear began to consume me. *Where was I going to get money? What was I going to do? How was I going to support myself? What about my poor crews and their families?*

One day while watching TV during lock down, I was sitting on my living room couch. I heard a voice. It said, "Laura, you now can do what you are called to do!" I looked around quickly searching to see if anyone else in the room had heard the voice. But the three sets of eyes fixed on the television screen in the corner of the room told me that in fact, they had not.

That voice led to a chain of events that set the trajectory of my current life in motion! What I did next was instrumental. I faced my fear and stepped out in faith. I told myself that . . .

*Up Until Now* . . . I was scared

*Up Until Now* . . . I was overwhelmed

*Up Until Now* . . . I was full of anxiety

*Up Until Now* . . . I was confused

*Up Until Now* . . . Life was living me and I was not living life

I was sick and tired of being sick and tired. Period. Over. Done! So, I acted!

Massive, empowered action born out of belief and faith. Over the past four years I had recognized patterns of success and had always loved mentoring and teaching! Without hesitation, I took a bold brave action step. I applied to be certified as a Transformational Life Coach. I was already an ICF Certified Coach and was seeing a couple of clients, but the Transformational Certification really resonated with me from a Faith standpoint. I stepped out in faith, enrolled, and was certified in Life Mastery principles.

Now, as I look back, without a doubt, the still small voice of

Truth that whispered in my ear that afternoon in the living room was guiding me. However, as I connected the dots looking backwards . . . this had nothing to do with me! NOTHING! It had everything to do with God. It was a calling. To serve and help others to find their purpose, passion, and their own calling in the human journey.

That brings us to this book. This amazing book, *Up Until Now*.

These pages are a labor of love that spans the greater part of two years. As I moved forward and began a private coaching practice, speaking and mentoring business full time, God/Universe blessed me with amazing clients—over one hundred of them in less than fifteen months. I learned so much from listening to their stories and journeys. It was remarkable to see them pick up and use the tools that were given to them and create *by design* a new life for themselves; One they LOVED living! They eradicated existing patterns of self-sabotaging and limitedness and replaced those patterns with empowered patterns that served them into gratitude and happiness. It was remarkable.

*Up Until Now* is a compilation of true stories from clients that were hurting, anxiety ridden, distraught and broken hearted *Up Until Now*. . . .

These amazing souls faced their fears and stepped out in Faith; mentally, physically, spiritually, emotionally, and financially. That decisiveness of action facilitated massive transformation in a positive way.

They just needed a voice to share their amazing stories! *Up Until Now* was born to serve them and give them a voice. These wonderful and inspiring stories are collected into one place with a heart of serving others out there that are hurting or lost.

I had the humble privilege of listening to these precious people overcome their obstacles. Time and time again, I was blown away by the sincerity and rawness of their situations and how it was transformed like a caterpillar to a butterfly right before my eyes.

I was the lucky one. I was the blessed girl that was able to witness soul after soul transform their lives.

So, herein lies the many stories from several of my current and previous clients and my family. Without a doubt, I know you will be inspired deep into your core as they openly share their true tales of overcoming and transforming.

Better grab a box of Kleenex, because you are going to need it!

—Laura K. Walker

LINDA WALKER
Keller, TX

## *The Gift*

> "Isaac prayed to the Lord for his wife, because she was barren. And the Lord granted his prayer, and his wife, Rebekah, conceived."
> —GENESIS 25:21

CHRISTMAS OF 1997 was the best for our family in many years. Three of our four daughters, their husbands, and our three grandsons were home to celebrate the joyous time of our Savior's birth with us. This was the first Christmas for our newest grandson, Benjamin, who would be four months old a few days after the holiday. Like all doting grandparents, we were guilty of going more than just a little overboard on all our grandson's gifts. In baby Benjamin's case, his gift (an ExerSaucer) wouldn't fit into his parent's sporty sedan, so I, volunteered to drive back to Arlington with them to help carry the Christmas goodies, and then go on to Frisco (north of Plano) to spend a few days with the fourth daughter, who hadn't been able to join us.

While in Frisco two days later on Benjamin's four-month birthday, my mobile phone rang. Cynthia, Benjamin's mother, was calling to inform us that Benjamin had been found dead in his crib at the babysitter's home. We were all in a state of shock and disbelief that such a precious, vibrant little boy could be snatched away so suddenly by SIDS.

The next few days were difficult for all of us, but our greatest concern was for Benjamin's parents. They were so young, and he was their first and only child. How unfair that this had happened to them. Being a Godly couple, they were surrounded by the thoughts and prayers of dozens of people. Many of us prayed that they would soon be blessed with another child—not to take Benjamin's place, but to fill the huge, gaping emptiness that his parents felt.

Mother's Day of '98 found us all together in Dallas. For my surprise, the girls had put together what I refer to as my "tribe necklace"—a chain strung with boy or girl, cat or dog, bootie or angel symbols in groupings, representing each of their families. Cynthia was appointed gift presenter, moving through the little symbols, each representing a daughter, husband, children, cats, and dogs, until finally she came to her own family. There was one for her husband, herself, an angel for our precious Benjamin, and a bootie for the new baby she announced was due in December! The ultimate Christmas 1998 gift for all of us . . . and surely an answered prayer.

> Dear Lord, we thank You for the gift of Your Son, Jesus, and we thank You for the gift of new life to our family. Most of all, we thank You for the assurance of the Psalmist, "The Lord hears when I call to Him." In Christ's name we pray. Amen.

**LORALEE BROER**
Aurora, CO

# Needle in a Haystack

MY HEART STARTED POUNDING faster as I frantically ripped through my bookbag looking for my wallet. Panic started to set in. A couple of hours earlier, I had stopped at an ATM to get my rent money, which meant my wallet was stuffed with hundreds of euros. It also contained my driver's license, debit and credit cards. Being in a foreign country without those items was definitely not a good thing.

It had been an amazing day until this moment. I had just finished traipsing all over Rome with my fellow students from my Master's program. We had had a memorable day drinking wine, eating good food, and enjoying the sights.

*Think, think, think . . . where did I last remember having my wallet?* We had eaten a typical Roman lunch at a small *trattoria* near our school. The next stop was the home of one of our fellow students houses for dessert and Prosecco on the other side of town, which required us to take several buses and a train. Then we walked through the winding cobblestone streets full of shops, ending up at our favorite coffee shop for espresso. Finally, we proceeded to one of the busiest tourist sites and hung out in the piazza by the famous Pantheon.

I could have dropped my wallet anywhere. The streets and piazza were packed with people. Or maybe one of the famous pickpockets had successfully lifted it from my bag when we were on one of the packed buses. *What was I going to do?* It wasn't even the thought of losing all my rent money that bothered me, but the fact that without my credit or debit card, I couldn't get any more money, and it would more than likely take at least a week to get new cards sent to me from the US. My mind was spinning as I mentally raced to all the places I had been to that day. I wasn't sure where to even start. And even if I did backtrack to all my previous destinations, the likelihood that someone had already found it and walked away with it was high.

I stood there in a debilitating panic until I told myself I needed to stay positive. I shook off my fear and jumped into action. I glanced at my best girlfriend and asked if she would go with me to backtrack our steps, and she agreed So, off we went to search for a needle in the haystack of Rome.

My intuition said to start back at the Pantheon. I walked with a skip in my step; I was determined to stay positive and visualize a good outcome.

As we walked down the narrow cobblestoned streets packed with people, I started telling my best friend a story of something that happened to me when I was a little girl.

My birthday is in March, and I would save my birthday money all year so I could buy my parents and brothers Christmas presents. One year, we were visiting some family friends in Germany and I was planning on buying my Christmas presents there, since Western Europe had nicer stores. My parents' friends had several children our age, and as you can imagine, we had a blast playing and riding bikes together. One evening, after a fun-filled day riding bikes all over town and through fields near their house, I realized my coin purse that had housed all my saved-up birthday money was gone. My heart sank and I burst into tears. My mother tried to comfort me. She said, "Loralee, why don't you pray, ask God to help you, and tomorrow, go look for it."

That night I prayed reverently that I would find my coin purse and even dreamt about my search. The next day, we went back to the fields to look for it. The fields were huge to my youthful self. We had ridden our bikes all over—it was, again, like looking for a needle in a haystack. I remember feeling determined, believing and trusting I would find it. The field's hay had been cut, but was still tall enough where you couldn't easily see through it. As I rode my bike through the field, I got close to a large, round haystack when something caught the corner of my eye. Tears once again filled my eyes as I looked down and saw my little pink Chinese designed coin purse. I could hardly believe my eyes! I jumped off my bike and scooped it up. It was a little wet from the dew and an animal had nibbled on one corner, but all my money was still inside! My heart was filled with joy—my prayers had worked. I still remember exactly what I bought my family members that Christmas; it turned out to be one of the most memorable Christmases ever!

I finished my story just as we arrived in the piazza by the Pantheon. I walked over to a section of wall I had sat on when we visited the area earlier. I looked around, my heart sinking when I didn't see it. I paused to regroup and drank in the sight around the piazza, watching what looked like thousands of people milling about.

All of a sudden, the crowds parted and I heard my name spoken in a thick accent as a man I didn't recognize walked up to me. I burst into tears and threw my arms around his neck before he could even finish what he was saying, for I knew the only way this stranger would know my name would be if he had found my wallet! He said he recognized me from my driver's license picture and handed me my wallet. He asked if everything was still in there, and it was! He then stated he had been lingering in the area for the last three to four hours looking for me.

The man explained that he was supposed to meet a friend and his friend was running late, and that he saw my wallet on the ground while he was waiting. He'd approached some police officers and tried to give them my wallet, but the officers declined to take it, saying if they did, then I would for sure never find it. (If you know, you know.) So, the good Samaritan decided to stay, in the hopes that I would come back looking for it. I insisted on giving him some money for his trouble—he'd missed having dinner with his friend to wait for me and postponed his own dinner—but he refused to take it, so I asked him to at least let me buy him a beer or glass of wine. He did agree to that, so we ventured to a little bar where we met up with a few of our fellow students.

We continued to exchange stories and get to know each other. Toward the end of the evening, as we prepared to go our separate ways, the good Samaritan declared that I was one of the most positive people he had ever met, and that our conversation had encouraged him deeply.

In the end, maintaining a positive attitude, listening to your intuition, honest people, having little girl faith, and being brave enough to look for a needle in a haystack turned a bad situation into an uplifting event with a rippling effect.

JUDY COOPER
Lake Oswego, OR

## *Inner Critic*

DAD, YOUR CONSTANT CRITICISM weighed heavily on me. So much that my shoulders slumped in shame, my head always hung low with eyes peering toward the ground, having seemingly given up any expectations of approval. Without any approval from you, I felt alone, made invisible by your silence. The only words I ever heard from you stung like a bee, then followed by feeling the pain of your disappointment in me, yet again.

    I thought when my fourth-grade teacher, Mrs. Nugent, acknowledged my talent for math by giving me an "A," that I would finally have achieved the status that you "see me" as worthy of encouragement. I was so excited to show you my report card and tell you about my grade, anxious but with such hardened certainty that this would be the one time I would get your approval . . . that you would be happy with me and my performance. Instead, your response was forever etched into my memory: "Why can't you get an A in *all* of your subjects?" The disappointment you expressed felt like a dagger searing straight through my heart, and my dream for your approval shattered! Once again, I'd disappointed you. After all, if an "A" didn't matter to you, then *I* didn't matter to you. That perception influenced my view of math, of my schoolwork, and of myself. The harshness of my father's words overshadowed my emotional health, which I shouldered well into adulthood.

At some point the concept of forgiveness was brought to my attention. I was intrigued enough to listen to the concept, along with listening to many stories of forgiveness. I was drawn into the idea of forgiveness, as my pain was too much to hold onto. I wanted to get rid of that burden . . . I wanted to heal. Forgiving you benefitted my own healing, so I forgave you for that moment and all the other moments when I longed for your attention but failed to get it.

I was certain at the time that I had forgiven you. Some twenty-five years later, I realized that there was still a portion of hurt that I was holding onto. I still felt invisible, so I took a deep breath and began searching inwardly, digging deeply for an answer. I found my nine-year-old self still blaming myself for *your* inability to "validate me," even when I got the "A." I blamed myself for thinking that I would get the recognition I deserved from you but in the end, didn't get. The strategy of "self-blame" has followed me on my life journey . . . *up until now*!

I forgave you many years ago for failing me as a parent, but realized my nine-year-old self was seeking forgiveness for thinking that my "A" grade would actually make a difference. I was hopeful that the "A" would be a turning point in our relationship. Instead, the "inner critic" was always ready to pounce on any perceived "failures," whether accurate perceptions or not. Constantly reminding me of my shortcomings kept me invisible and powerless . . . *up until now*! Once I recognized the need to take responsibility for the "emotional triggers" that still impacted me, I began forgiving myself for my imperfections, whether real or imagined. Once I took the action of forgiving myself, I was able to take back the story that had been dominating my life, my nine-year-old self was no longer invisible to me, no longer held power over me. I have rewritten that story on who I was then into who I am *now*. I stopped believing what I was saying about myself and began providing myself with the love I was never given from you. I so deserve it!

I take a moment each day to review the moments I feel I deserve recognition for. Every time I text "thinking of you," or "I love you," or just a smiley face, I am creating a meaningful moment. Each moment I stay calm when surrounded by "noise" deserves to be validated, because it is a display of who I am today!

STEVE DOTSON, DC
Colleyville, TX

## *The Seeds of My Becoming*

MAY 7, 1991, BASIC TRAINING CHARLIE COMPANY 795
MILITARY POLICE BATTALION, ANNISTON, ALABAMA

"Drill Sergeant! Private Dotson requests permission to speak!" I barked at my commander.

"Speak!" barked back Drill Sergeant Landrum.

"Can our platoon have more iodine tablets to clean our water bottles? They smell like mildew," I requested with no emotional efficacy.

Drill Sergeant Landrum curtly replied, "Dr. Nissan!" (He named me Nissan because my last name, Dotson, sounded like the auto maker's now-defunct brand name, Datsun.) Trying to keep the platoon healthy, huh? Well, drop and give me twenty!" [pushups]

I thought to myself . . . *doctor?* I never considered myself doctor material, but at that moment, the title "doctor" sounded much better than "private!" I didn't realize it at that moment, but Drill Sergeant Landrum had planted a seed in the fertile ground of my subconscious, of being more than I thought I could be. It was a thought that stuck with me and eventually shaped my life drastically.

I enjoyed my time in the army and was given the opportunity to meet great people and see much of Europe, Asia Minor, and the Middle East. On one occasion, I was on temporary duty at Incirlik Airbase in Adana, Turkey. For some reason I had a headache after I got off the plane, but I just sucked it up and drove on. I went to the barbershop to get a haircut. The Turkish local sat me in his chair and did a great job cutting my hair. We made some small talk, and then he rolled out the red carpet! He washed my hair, shaved my neck, and massaged my shoulders! It felt great, but that wasn't all. He noticed I couldn't turn my head very well, so then he told me to relax as he wrapped a towel around my neck.

Not knowing what he planned to do, I said, "Hold on! What are you doing?"

"Something that will help you turn your head better. Just relax."

He made some quick, controlled moves, first left and then right. I heard the loudest pops in my neck and thought I'd been sent to another dimension! Sure enough, I could turn my head so much easier, and after a few minutes my headache was gone. It was a $3 haircut, and I tipped him an extra $10. Wow, I thought, I need to get that done more often! I felt so much better. I felt . . . alive! Then it occurred to me, wouldn't it be cool to do that for a living? I could help so many people move well and feel great! I knew it would take more education, because in America, licensed chiropractors and osteopaths perform adjustments/manipulative treatments, not barbers. And at that moment, another seed was sown . . . Be-ing of more service to others.

Although I proudly served for seven years, I left the army with certain physical conditions that were aggravated by mental factors, such as internal conflict/stress, that I didn't want anyone to know about. I thought that anyone who knew about these issues would consider me "damaged goods" and that if my secret was discovered I wouldn't be able to get a decent job. I even tried medicating myself with prescription drugs, alcohol, and cigarettes to deal with my issues, but soon realized I was only covering up my symptoms. I still get queasy, reading the list of side effects from the medications! Most of the side effects were worse than the problem they were trying to fix! I'm not saying *all* medications are bad. There's a time and place for everything. It was simply a lifestyle choice I decided not to continue to make.

## SEPTEMBER–OCTOBER 2001. THE WET SEASON, CẨM ĐƯỜNG, LONG THÀNH DISTRICT, DONG NAI, VIETNAM

My mother took my brother and I on a trip to Vietnam to see her homeland and visit our relatives. It was my first time there. It was beautiful. The tropical fruits and vegetables my family grew on their property were vibrant, exotic, and delicious. When traveling abroad, it's recommended to boil water before drinking, avoid using ice cubes in drinks, and to eat thoroughly cooked foods vs. eating raw foods, etc. Well, I didn't follow any of those recommendations! I was immersing myself in Vietnamese cuisine and wanted to try everything. There were no kitchen or dining room tables at my grandparents' house. We all sat on the floor to eat. I could deal with that, but I couldn't handle not having air conditioning. The weather was getting the best of me. It was very hot, extremely humid, and constantly raining! Drinking Tiger Beer and homemade cognac didn't make things better. Dehydration was something I constantly battled and ultimately lost after just eight days in the country.

Although I had taken the recommended shots and malaria pills, I was down! Sick with the flu, or some other unidentified ailment. We rode from the village into Bien Hoa on mopeds, zigzagging around holes in the muddy dirt road and busy city streets, to get to the closest infirmary for another shot in the bottom of I don't know what! For several nights, I had bouts of shivering, sweats, and diarrhea. My muscles were so stiff and tight that I thought they were going to rip off my bones. I felt as if I was on my deathbed, with an elephant standing on me. On top of that, I was having nightmares.

My grandparents donated some land to the church next door to their house. In front of the church was a large tree with a statue of Mother Mary at the base, crying tears of blood. The statue could easily be seen out of my grandparents' bathroom window (I was there many times). I asked why she was crying. My mother said that Mary wept tears of blood as she prayed over lost souls. With that in the back of my delirious mind, I began battling demons, thinking they were trying to possess me. I redirected my attention and began praying for God to deliver me from this sickness.

My uncle worked as a cab driver during the day and came to visit me because he heard I was sick. Like an angel sent from above, he began treating me with acupuncture, cupping, gua sha, and most notably, spinal adjustments. I could not believe the relief I felt after those treatments. I begged my mom to ask my uncle to come back the next day to treat me again. The spinal adjustments made me feel like I was getting my life back! The muscle aches, stiffness, and tightness all went away. Another seed was sown, and that was when I discovered my purpose in life! So, I said a prayer and made a commitment. "Dear God, if you let me live, I will go back home and become a chiropractor!"

DECEMBER 12, 2009: GRADUATION DAY, SHERMAN COLLEGE OF CHIROPRACTIC, SPARTANBURG, SOUTH CAROLINA

As I walked across the stage to receive my diploma, an overwhelming feeling of gratitude came over me, grateful for the people and experiences in my life that led me here. This was the day chiropractic medicine became the vehicle I use to humbly serve others. I knew I was blessed to do something I love and call it work.

> "Success is . . . knowing your purpose in life, growing to reach your maximum potential, and sowing seeds that benefit others."
> —JOHN C. MAXWELL

KIRSTEN FAGAN
Semmes, AL

## *Life is a Gift*

*Beep! Beep! Beep!*

The fire alarm startled me awake. I groaned, "Not again!" and pulled my pillow over my head. It was after 3:00am, and I was so tired. I was a college student living in a dormitory. All I wanted to do was eat, sleep (mostly sleep), and go to class.

*Urgh, why does that fire alarm have to keep going off?* This was probably the third or even fourth time it had happened this month. I was so annoyed. *Didn't they know college students need their rest?* And to make matters worse, this was the week of our final exams for the semester.

I laid there a few moments contemplating burrowing under my covers and hiding from the RA (Resident Advisor), but something inside me wouldn't let me do it. Maybe it was a voice, or maybe it was a feeling, but something made me get out of my bed.

Mumbling with frustration, I threw back my covers and got up. I figured we would be back in the dorm in a few minutes, so I skipped grabbing a jacket, slid on my flip-flops, grabbed my cellphone—which was never far from me—and for some reason I also grabbed my car keys. I found my friends in the hall, and we all sleepily exited the building.

It was a chilly April night, so I tried to move around to keep warm, hoping we wouldn't be outside for long . . . But on this particular night it was different, and it seemed to be taking longer than normal.

Then I realized that the Dean and the RA's kept counting the girls. Had they lost count? Had someone stayed in the dorm like I had wanted to do? What was taking so long? It seemed like they repeated the count at least three times, maybe more. I rolled my eyes and hoped they would hurry up so we could go back inside.

Pretty soon it became clear that we weren't getting back in the building anytime soon. I didn't know what was going on, but I was so cold. So were my friends, most of whom had also come out without jackets or socks. We were all shivering.

Suddenly it dawned on me that I had my car keys. Why not go sit in my car and run the heat? I walked over to where the Dean and other staff members stood and asked the Dean if a four of us could sit in my car to get warm. She agreed, on the condition that we not leave the campus.

It all seemed like a joke as we sat in my car and watched everyone standing around waiting. Someone joked that maybe someone burned their popcorn and maybe the firefighters couldn't get the alarm to shut off. We continued to laugh and talk, but it was taking way too long.

Then we all noticed a red glow above the dorm building and then we began to see smoke pouring into the sky. We made a collective gasp.

The building really was on fire.

The inside of the car went quiet as we realized it wasn't a joke anymore. The next couple of hours were a blur . . .

Eventually, we were told that if we had friends or family who lived off campus, to see if we could spend the night with them, and we would be updated in the morning.

My brain was foggy as I tried to figure out what to do. I realized I was the only one with family in the area, a cousin of my dad's, and knew my friends didn't have anywhere they could go.

I quickly called my dad's cousin, and she graciously allowed myself and my three friends to stay at her house. That was such a relief, because we were exhausted. We felt so grateful to have a warm place to stay rather than having to stand on the lawn outside the dorm wondering where we would go. We had nothing but the clothes on our backs, and we were so thankful to have a warm place to sleep.

The next morning, we drove back to the school, hoping to find out what was going on and to see if we could pick up some of our clothes. We shared jokes about how lucky we were not to have to sleep in our birthday suits, but we were quite anxious to get fresh clothes.

By mid-morning we were notified that morning classes had been canceled and that we would be allowed in the dorm to pick up clothes and other belongings, but no decision had been made beyond that.

It wasn't long before whispers began. According to the grapevine, not everyone had made it out of the building and something bad had happened. News began to spread, and finally it was confirmed that there had, in fact, been a death in the fire.

We were shocked at this news and wondered who it could be, but no other details were released. The news finally came in toward the end of the day: one student was dead and two others remained hospitalized.

Final exams were canceled, one after the other. By the following morning we were told that all finals were canceled, and they were asking everyone to pack their things and go home.

As the news began releasing pictures of the girls who'd been hurt or killed in the fire, I felt a jumble of emotions. Guilt, sadness, gratitude, thankfulness, guilt again, and so many other emotions. I felt a great desire to get out of there, so I quickly packed up my room, loaded up my car, and drove home. The drive took seven hours, but I didn't want to stick around.

I didn't understand my feelings, and I'm not sure I do even now. But I was grateful for listening to that small voice that told me to get up and get out. While the fire didn't make it to my side of the dorm, the reality was nevertheless sobering: It could have been me in the fire.

When we returned to school, we held a memorial service in the butterfly garden on campus dedicated to the girl who lost her life. Student services was offering counseling, and heaviness hung in the air.

Now, when I think about that moment in time, my mind fills with questions. Why her? What force spares one life and takes another? And while I don't know the answers, I am very grateful for one more reminder of just how precious life is. I'm thankful for my life. As I think back to that moment of, *Should I get up or should I stay in my bed?* I am so grateful for that small voice telling me to get up and for my life being spared. Life is a gift, and I will do my very best to live it to the fullest.

## DAWN L. HARGRAVES, ESQ.
Bay Port, NY

# *FFMG*

I GREW UP in a middle-class neighborhood, in an ordinary home with my parents and younger brother. My father worked as an insurance salesman and my mother was a stay-at-home mom. By all accounts, my family appeared to the outside world as an average American family; however, no one knew the terror that existed within the walls of that ordinary-looking home. You see, my father was an alcoholic who was physically and emotionally abusive, not only to me, but also to my mother and brother. Coming home, we never knew what we would walk into.

    I distinctly remember holding the handle of the screen door and taking a deep breath before I pushed in the button on the handle to open it, trying to prepare myself mentally for whatever awaited me on the other side. I never knew whether the family would be sitting at the kitchen table calmly eating dinner, or whether my father would be in a rage, hitting my mother with a leather belt or holding her hostage with a shotgun. It was very scary and confusing.

    As I grew up, I never felt like I fit in anywhere. I was uncomfortable in my own skin, always seeking ways to calm my internal uneasiness. When I was thirteen, my girlfriend, Lorraine, and I stole a gallon of cheap wine from my house and snuck into the woods to drink it. My first sip was miraculous—the tart taste and warm sensation the alcohol created as it traveled down my throat . . . and then the miracle. The worries in my head turned off, replaced by an instant sense of calm and then the feeling of belonging. All that from a drink. I thought I had found my solution. As a result, I drank again and again, and each time I drank, I drank more and more—doing all I could to quell the turmoil in my head. The more I drank, the more I wanted to drink and the more I *did* drink—often to the point of blacking out.

As I continued to drink in this uncontrolled, unstoppable manner, bad things started to happen to me. I became isolated from my friends and family. The peace alcohol initially provided to my ever-rattling brain began to fade. I felt more desperate than ever, to the point where I actually wanted to die. Every time I drove over a bridge or an overpass, all I could think about was driving off of it and crashing.

At the age of twenty-seven, I moved in with a guy I had met at a local bar. We bonded almost instantly, and once again I felt as though I was going to be OK. But after nine months together, he informed me that he believed he had a problem with alcohol. My initial thought was, *how could he have a problem with alcohol, when I drink so much more than him?* My second thought—the one I said aloud—was, "Don't worry, I know exactly what to do." You see, people had been telling me about Alcoholics Anonymous for years. I had been given numerous AA literature, and I even knew where the local meetings were held. I told him I had a solution for him, and the next day I brought him to his first Alcoholics Anonymous meeting. He fell in love with AA and AA fell in love with him. I, however, did not feel the same. AA was great for him, but I insisted *I* wasn't the one with the alcohol problem.

We continued to live together, but as he got more and more

sober, I became increasingly resentful of his newfound freedom from the grip of dependency. After about a year, he informed me that I had to either stop drinking or move out. I had never felt so desperate and so alone. I had nowhere else to go. The next morning, he brought me to my first AA meeting. I insisted we travel to a meeting more than forty-five minutes from our home because I didn't want anyone to know I was an alcoholic. You see, I had become everything I swore I wouldn't.

By the grace of God, the obsession to drink was immediately removed and I began to follow the suggestions made to me by the gracious and loving women of AA. As I began to work the program of AA to clear the wreckage and guilt of my past, I slowly let these women into my heart. They loved me back to health and I eventually became comfortable in my own skin—no longer looking to fill from the outside in. Sobriety delivered what the alcohol had promised.

This was not the end of the journey. In AA, it is strongly suggested that you find a Higher Power. For me, I had always believed in God and had little difficulty believing in God as I understood Him. Notwithstanding my belief in God, there was still something missing from my life.

After my mother, my best friend, and another woman who had been like a mother to me died, and my long-term relationship ended—all events within three months of each other—I again found myself feeling overwhelmed and lost. Again, I felt as though I didn't belong, and the rejection I felt was killing me. After twenty-eight years of sobriety, I again found myself thinking about ending my life.

Again, by the grace of God and with the assistance of the people in AA, I figured out what was wrong. The solution, you see, was inside me. I was grateful to God for having removed my obsession to drink alcohol, but I had refused to let God into any of the other areas of my life. I was raised to be self-sufficient and was determined to do everything on my own. It was out of this darkness that I again walked into the light. I believed in God and now I started to rely on God in all areas. What a freedom! I again feel as though I belong and that I am part of something much bigger than myself. I Finally Found My God (FFMG).

DIANA CHERRYN KELLY, PHD
Dubai, UAE

## *This World to the Next: Who Says They Don't Live On?*

I THOUGHT it was almost ridiculous that she could be so generous.

"Wow, those throw pillows are so unique, such beautiful colors. Where did you get them?"

"Here, they're yours!"

My mother was known for her kindness and generosity. In my teenage years, I didn't get it. But eventually, the living sample of my parents' faith and values left a profound impression on me and provided the basis for my foundational beliefs in God and for reaching out to those around me. Little did I know, these same values would rub off on my siblings and me when we became adults with families of our own.

In my later teen years, I found my connection with God and Jesus through a series of encounters and experiences. This brought to life the Bible verse:

> *"Love God with all your heart, soul, and mind, and love your neighbor as yourself. There are no commandments greater than these,"* said Jesus.
>
> —MARK 12:30–31

I stood at the crossroads of life as I graduated with a Bachelor of Science degree, ready to embark on my career. I had always been hardworking, determined, and ambitious, striving to do better each day. My goal was to climb the corporate ladder and become a successful professional. At the same time, I felt a tug on my heartstrings to go in a completely different direction. What if I could do something to help those in need and make the world a better place? I started feeling that my purpose and mission in life were different from the one I had originally envisioned. Even if I turned out to be highly successful in the corporate world, I felt that I might look back years later and regret that I had missed my life's highest purpose. I didn't think I could live with that, and so I chose the unconventional path.

One of my favorite quotes is:

> "Be the change you want to see in the world."
> —MAHATMA GANDHI

Drawing on personal experience, I have learned that when you change your own life, it impacts the lives of those around you through your loving service and sample. So instead of going corporate, I interned with a local organization in the culturally colorful and modern city of Kuala Lumpur, in Malaysia (my home country), learning about casework and the many ways to add value to individuals and communities.

Soon after, I met a musically inclined, smart, funny, and adorable young Irish American gentleman named Edward James (fondly known as Ed), who shared my aspirations. Living in Singapore at the time, he worked with the US Refugee Program, processing Vietnamese refugees to the United States. Ed was already well immersed in being a public servant and had been giving back in the neighboring countries. He won my heart with his charming ways, and we fell in love and married.

Together we partnered with charitable organizations to render educational and public service to the many cities, countries, and geographic regions where we lived over the years, from Singapore to Hong Kong, South America, England, India, Southeast Asia, and then on to the Middle East and the Arabian Gulf. We lived and worked with people of all races, religions, and cultures and learned patience, tolerance, and respect for the diverse and wonderful mix of peoples around the world. Together we learned that the basic needs of mankind are basically the same all over the world—our need for love, acceptance, forgiveness, and enriching relationships, plus the need for security, safety, and providence.

Our four beautiful children were born in different countries—Malaysia, Argentina, Thailand, and the Holy Land. Ours was a life filled with love and harmony which gave emotional and psychological stability to our core family unit. I attribute it to both the inspiring work we shared in reaching out to others, bettering their lives physically, emotionally, and academically, while inviting others into our family circle.

We found ourselves in incredibly exciting but sometimes risky, dangerous, and life-threatening situations. We were in Buenos Aires during the Falkland war, amidst riots and demonstrations on the streets. When the second Palestinian Intifada hit, we found ourselves with helicopters whirring overhead and bullets and rockets flying over our home, as we lived close to a Jewish settlement in the mixed territories of Israel. Ambulance sirens constantly blared as they brought the injured to hospitals, crossing multiple military checkpoints to get from one town to another in the West Bank, with snipers watching closely in case a wrong move was made. There seemed to be a divine protection present watching over us, perhaps honoring the sacrificial work to which we had dedicated our lives.

The extreme poverty in some countries, and the pain and

suffering in war-torn lands, were heartbreaking. We worked with others to bring aid, food, clothing, and supplies to destitute families. We organized a dynamic therapy through a music and drama program for young teens and children throughout the West Bank and the Gaza Strip. Performed by an international youth group, the program bridged differences and helped overcome the fear and trauma these young Palestinians had experienced in the war zone. They had so little normalcy in their lives—toys, games, books, school supplies, and carefree experiences were a rarity. Instead, they watched endless news on the television about war and conflict, death, pain, and sorrow.

We worked in refugee camps and with disadvantaged communities in the Middle East and North Africa (MENA) region, particularly in the West Bank, Jordan, Syria, Lebanon, and Iraq. Prompted to meet the dire needs we witnessed firsthand, we established an Educational Consultancy, a social enterprise in the United Arab Emirates (UAE), assisted by a small team. Dubai is a flourishing business capital in the region, and our vision was to connect aid and build capacity for the communities and families in neighboring war-torn lands. Now, fourteen years later, we can say that this vision is being fulfilled.

When we began our work in the UAE, we were asked by many, "What are you going to do for our country?" This propelled us into nationwide research in 2008, which revealed the need for motivational, life skills, and extra-curricular education programs for children and youth in the UAE.

Therefore, we initiated a program to bring high-value educational courses, aligned to the goals of the Ministry of Education, to under-resourced schools. Courses included career development, information technology literacy, financial capability, environmental awareness, and Science, Technology, Education, and Math (STEM) topics for older children and youth. We also launched a series of Early Childhood Development courses, Start Early, in partnership with Boeing Middle East (ME) for young mothers and teachers. The program was operational in the Gulf countries of Qatar, Kuwait, Oman, and the UAE for three consecutive years. In partnership with international and regional corporate companies, these courses are provided at no cost to the under-resourced schools we serve, along with material aid to build capacity for their classroom spaces.

Things were moving ahead, just as we had hoped. Unbeknownst to us, events that would turn our lives upside down were just around the corner.

Ed and I were two years into our work in the UAE, healthy and physically strong individuals, and celebrating our thirtieth year of marriage. One day, Ed experienced some mild chest pains. The medical tests showed that he had a slight blockage in his arteries, but the doctor assured us that it was of no immediate cause for concern, saying we could do an angiogram at some point in the future.

We decided to go ahead with the angiogram sooner than later. However, a couple of days before the scheduled procedure, Ed experienced much stronger pains in his chest, and as we rushed him to the hospital—he lost consciousness! I held him in my arms and practiced all the emergency first aid I knew. Upon reaching the hospital, three doctors immediately began attempting to resuscitate him. Twenty minutes later, I stood in disbelief as the doctors delivered the most tragic news ever . . . my beloved Ed was gone! Gone! My mind didn't want to accept it. *How can that be true? He had been healthy, strong, and active just an hour ago. And now he's gone?*

My initial reaction was to blame God. I wondered if the God I loved and had served did indeed exist and if so, why would He allow this sudden passing of my beloved husband? And without a sign or warning?

It was truly a difficult and heart-wrenching phase for me, and

I found myself yet again at another of life's crossroads. *What now?* How could I possibly carry on as a single mother with my eighteen-year-old son, Steve, ready to go to university, and my youngest, Kyla, only ten? Should I leave my work in this foreign country, go back to my home country and secure a more stable job? Or should I stay on and continue?

It was a major life-changing decision to make. I fell asleep conflicted about what to do, when this scene unfolded before me in a dream: My husband and I were living in the home of a local family. During the night, a violent storm hit, and we awakened to see water levels rising all around us in the house. We immediately went into rescue mode, bailing the water with buckets and taking the children to higher ground. I saw my husband smiling and nodding his head at me. I knew that was a signal, an answer to my question. My mission would be to continue our service to those in need in this country. That dream gave me the faith and conviction that my work was not done and that I needed to continue, despite the challenges I faced.

Looking back now, twelve years later, I can attest that this was the best decision I could have made. I put my mind and heart back into public service, determined to not allow myself to wallow in self-pity, nor to be drowned in lamenting my loss, but to continue to move forward. With God's grace, I learned to stand on my own, shoring up weaker areas of my life or those where I had been dependent upon Ed.

I also put my best efforts into supporting my two youngest children. Through a series of miracles and the support of loyal friends and scholarships, my daughter attended a prestigious British private school, while my son went on to the University of North Texas to earn his undergrad degree in engineering.

Though I missed Ed tremendously, things were coming together for me. I had the blessing of continuing to see him in my dreams on numerous occasions. Through this understanding, he reassured me that he had not disappeared into oblivion, but had moved on to a whole new world of living and meaning. My faith rebounded, and though I did not understand why God had to take him, I found peace in knowing that Ed had gone on to a higher calling.

It all made sense, for Ed to be chosen for a higher calling. To me and the others who knew him, Ed had been a living saint—a gentle, warm, loving, kind, and caring person, smart, gifted in music, songwriting, and languages, and yet so humble. And I had had the blessing of living with Ed, loving and serving others with him, for thirty years. Is there really anything more that I could have asked for?

It appears I wasn't quite done being in the "wringer." Almost exactly two years later, I received more earth-shattering news. I got a phone call from my brother in the States, informing me that Steve, my twenty-year-old son, had been involved in an accident and did not survive. He was gone, too.

The news had me reeling in disbelief. Steve had just completed his first year of college with honors and had such a bright future ahead of him. I immediately began to feel my whole world crumbling around me for a second time. "Not again," I told myself as I made arrangements to fly to the States. My life had been filled with love and happiness, starting with loving and caring parents, then a wonderful husband, then beautiful children, and a fantastic life of travel and service. I was not ready spiritually nor emotionally for another traumatic incident after losing Ed, and it felt as though my heart could not handle this grief. Mothers should never have to bury their children, and I struggled to cope with the resultant grief, depression, and psychosomatic state that one in this position would naturally experience.

First, soon after Steve's passing, I had a vivid dream. In it,

Steve was standing with me in the kitchen next to a basket of fruit. He reached down, took a banana, and started eating it, "Hey Steve, you can't eat bananas; you're allergic to them," I said. He looked at me, and with a smile, replied, "I'm okay now, Mom. I'm fine."

Then came another out-of-this-world occurrence: The doorbell rang, and when I opened the door, there stood Ed with Steve beside him holding a huge bouquet of flowers. In mental telepathic communication, Steve told me that he loved and cherished me dearly and was so sorry for the grief I was suffering. Ed assured me, "Don't worry, I've got him." Whether this was a dream or a vision I'm not sure of, but it did give me great comfort and the peace I sorely needed. I had my twelve-year-old in the house with me, and I thought to myself, *And I've got her.* I determined right then to be strong and to be there for her.

The pain stayed as a sword piercing my heart, but I knew I couldn't allow self-pity to overtake me, and so I claimed Heaven's grace to see me through. I knew that I needed to sink my teeth into something greater than myself, something substantial to occupy my mind. I signed on to a doctorate program in higher education, one that aligned with my experience with working to alleviate child poverty through education.

Six years after Steve's passing, I walked onstage to receive my Doctorate in Education. In recent years, I have received the "United Nations International Women's Day Award" in Abu Dhabi for my years of public service. I have spoken at multiple women's program events and was interviewed for a television show about my work as well as overcoming traumatic incidents in our lives. My work and social projects have been featured in local newspapers. I feel deeply humbled, yet honored by this recognition for my lifelong work. I am grateful for the generous and kind words of countless individuals who affirmed that my support has been strengthened and enriched their lives.

From this world to the next: Who says the departed don't live on? Though I still don't understand God's reasons for calling my husband and son home, I have to believe that God knows best. Perhaps they are needed for a mission higher than the one here . . . perhaps they bridge a gap between our two worlds. I see them in my dreams often, and now I have the comfort of knowing they are my earthly angels watching out for us.

ELLEN MOSELEY-MAY
Livingston, TX

## Setting Down the Weight

I WAS NINE YEARS OLD when my teacher said to me, "Ellen, I need you to go to the office," I felt a warm sensation fill my body. Everyone at our lunch table looked at me as if I had committed an unspeakable crime and was being escorted to jail like a criminal. In the 1970's, getting in trouble at school was a big deal. Huge! We didn't turn in homework late, didn't misbehave in class, talk back to our teachers, and we certainly didn't get called to the principal's office. My heart was racing, my palms were sweaty, and I was absolutely certain my face was as red as the apple I had given my teacher the day before.

As I stood up, I remembered that my Aunt Pam had allowed me to bring her baton to school so I could play with it at recess. Most of my friends had their own, but I didn't. Aunt Pam had made me promise not to lose it, as she'd had it since she was on the high school drill team and it was special to her. Not wanting it to be confiscated during my impending doom of an office visit, I handed it to my friend Katherine and asked her to keep it safe. My teacher gently led me down the hall with her hand on the back of my neck. She didn't speak or give any indication as to what I had done to get into trouble. As soon as we stepped into the office, I saw several teachers and office staff noticeably upset and my mom standing there waiting for me, her face red and swollen from crying. My fears of being in trouble vanished, the fear remained. Something was terribly wrong.

My mom said, "Ellen, I'm so sorry, but your Aunt Pam has been attacked. She's hurt pretty badly and is in the hospital." Upon hearing her words, I lost all control, and I broke down in wrenching sobs. That was the moment my life changed forever.

His name was Johnny Paul Penry. Johnny was a shy child, with piercing brown eyes. Labeled mentally retarded by testing, he struggled academically in his childhood. Many people, including his school counselors, agreed that was probably the reason for the social difficulties he also had. As Johnny matured into adolescence, he exhibited escalating antisocial behaviors which prompted his being sent to the Mexia State School. When he was released at the age of sixteen, he functioned at a somewhat normal level, although he was technically illiterate, self-centered, and shallow. Leading an aimless and often unsupervised life, Johnny gave in to his violent side within a year, committing his first of several rapes at age seventeen. He was in and out of prison for multiple rapes over the next few years. In 1979, he was granted parole, and less than three months after his release, he raped and murdered my Aunt Pam.

Over the next thirty years, I found myself on a rollercoaster ride of anger, resentment, and unforgiveness. I carried the weight of what was taken from me for almost three decades, and it rotted me from the inside, tantamount to if I'd drank poison for breakfast daily. I attended countless hearings, trials, Supreme Court sessions, competency hearings, television interviews, and congressional hearings throughout those years, fighting for justice for my aunt. All fueled by my hatred for a man I had never met. It's crazy how I had allowed one act of a stranger to completely consume my life. Each time I would face a legal proceeding, I would allow my anger to take over and would put the full weight of it toward one purpose—making sure John Penry was executed for the pain he had caused my family.

By 2008, John Penry had been tried, convicted of murder, and given the death penalty three times. We had to retry him due to appeals, and my resolve was wearing very thin.

By this time, I had become a wife and mother, and my daughter, Pamela, couldn't really understand my anger. Much had happened with our case during her short fifteen years of life, but it all culminated into one moment when we were faced with having to go to trial for a fourth time. We were faced with the decision to continue to allow the hatred to control us, or to let go of it all and decide once and for all that we were going to move forward and let go of the weight that was John Penry. We chose the latter and settled on a plea bargain that would end the battle for good.

The death penalty was taken off the table. The day I gave my victim impact statement and we finalized the plea bargain, Pamela came to me in tears, saying she was worried about him going to Hell. She said she felt guilty because she didn't think she should feel bad for him. She didn't know the great-aunt for whom she had been named, but she had seen me struggle through the years. In that moment, I realized my daughter had become a victim in her own generation, and yet, she was choosing love in place of hate. She was worried that I would be upset with her for feeling bad for my aunt's murderer, but the truth was that I was relieved. Up until that moment, I wouldn't allow myself to let go because I was afraid to be unfaithful to Aunt Pam's memory. I felt a relief to know that someone was brave enough to say out loud that it was okay to forgive. Secretly I had wanted to for years, but it took the innocent heart of a child to show me how. I needed someone to tell me I could do it without it being a betrayal to my aunt. My teenage daughter gave me the perspective I needed to set down that weight, once and for all.

In that moment I knew I had done all I could to demonstrate my love for my aunt. Letting go was allowed. I was sure it was time to forgive and so, I did. I released myself from the chains that had been keeping me a prisoner outside of prison walls, as much as John Penry was a prisoner inside those walls. That night I thanked God for the experience and knowledge I gained through the long process of transforming my hate, and for the first time ever, I prayed for John Penry and went to bed. Tomorrow I would begin a new life without the weight of hatred.

Today, I can honestly say I don't hate John Penry. I don't wish him death. I don't want him to go to Hell. I pray one day he will realize that he is a child of God, loved and worthy of forgiveness, and that if he is willing, he, too, can be a force for good in the world.

APRIL MAZZONI
Littleton, CO

# *Oops, I did it, again! (breathe . . .)*

Hello, I'm April, and I have something to get off my chest . . .

My story begins with . . . well, me of course. I was a young teenager who had run away from home and found myself pregnant at nineteen, by a man I loved. Unfortunately, that young love didn't work out. However, there's a positive part to my story—we are friends now and co-parent extremely well.

No need to worry, then I met "The man of my dreams . . ." Ha-ha. That's right, the proverbial man of my dreams.

After a whirlwind romance, seventeen months later, I learned I was pregnant with twins. I was terrified and happy at the same time. Things were good, and I was excited at the thought of welcoming new little ones into the world. But not long into my pregnancy, tragedy raised its head . . . I lost one of my twins. Even with my sadness, I was so incredibly grateful that one of my babies survived, a beautiful girl. Her father and I had a long twelve-year relationship before breaking up. Those twelve years with the "man of my dreams" hadn't played out as I had anticipated. Instead, they were filled with emotional and physical abuse, cheating, lying and a hell of a lot of loneliness—I constantly felt alone. He was an alcoholic, which brought with it another set of challenges for our family that were not positive. I tried very hard to help him with his addiction throughout our years together. After all, isn't that what true love does?

I found myself sitting at home one evening with my newborn baby girl and my little guy, waiting for my man to come home . . . after all, it had been hours since he'd gotten off work. I repeatedly phoned him. No answer, no texts, nothing. As the hours passed with no word from him, my emotions escalated into anxiety, panic, worry, and dread all mixed together. My mind was racing. *Is he just out with his friends and ignoring me, or did he get into an accident? Am I ever going to see him again?*

As I soon found out the reason for his not coming home or calling, I was devastated. It was brought to light that he'd left work with a female coworker with whom he'd been having an affair. He did this, leaving me home alone with my one-year-old son and our brand-new baby girl, worried about his wellbeing. My dream man had become, in fact, a walking nightmare.

But as we do sometimes, I forgave him for his indiscretion, and we worked on our relationship and our family. Everything was very good for a while. We moved forward with our lives, the babies grew, and two years flew by.

During those two years, we moved our family of four into a cute little apartment while continuing to work on our relationship and family. By all outside appearances, things were good. We were at least heading in a direction that felt better, more positive. One day we were out running errands and we ran into a friend of his, whom he hadn't seen in years. We chatted and wound up inviting the friend back to our place to play cards and have some drinks. He began to tell us about his girlfriend. He told us that she had two kids, but he wasn't really in love with her and didn't want to be with her, but couldn't bring himself to break it off with her because he felt bad about doing so. I explained to him that even though I didn't know the woman, he wasn't being fair to her. I suggested that he tell her how he really felt, so she could have a chance to find true happiness and love with someone else. The evening ended, and the friend went home.

Within a few weeks, this friend began to hang out with us more frequently and he began to bring his girlfriend along, obviously ignoring our earlier talk. Regardless, the four of us became remarkably close friends. We had many good evenings full of laughter and fun. His girlfriend and I became inseparable. Then one day, tragedy hit both of us simultaneously. Her grandma died, and I had a heartbreak of my own to face.

My heart broke for her and the loss she'd suffered, but I was also hurting and in need of some sympathy. My "dream man" dropped an emotional bomb on me, sending me back into nightmare mode. He said he needed space and was going to stay with his uncle for a little while until he got himself together. He told me he loved me, and the separation wouldn't be permanent, he just needed to be alone for a while. I was crushed. I called my friend to tell her about it, but her phone was turned off. *This is odd*, I thought. I really needed to talk to her, but couldn't reach her.

A few days later, my fiancé came over to spend time with our daughter and to see me. I told him I couldn't get hold of my girlfriend and was concerned about her. We decided to go to the store to get a few things. I was driving, and a voice inside me whispered, "Go to her house." So, I planted my hands firmly on the steering wheel and drove directly to my friend's house with my fiancé and kids riding along. They didn't know we were going there until we were close to her house. I explained that I needed to check on her real quick since I hadn't heard from her and her phone wasn't working. Her cousin answered the door and told me my friend was at her grandma's funeral. The cousin added that my friend had plans for afterward so she wouldn't be home for a while.

I asked if I could leave a note for her because her phone still wasn't working. The cousin let me into the house to write a note. I went inside the house, found a pen and paper in her bedroom, and proceeded to write her a note: *I miss you so, so much and I am more than sorry about your grandma. You know I am here for you ANYTIME. I love you. Call me!* I signed my name and left the note on her nightstand, and as I got up to leave, I glanced into her open closet and saw all my fiancé's clothes in it. I could not believe my eyes. It literally sucked the breath right out of my chest. Then I noticed boxer shorts on a corner of her bed . . . and I recognized those as belonging to him.

I pulled out a photo of my fiancé and asked her cousin if she knew this guy. "Yes," she replied, "that's my cousin's boyfriend." I couldn't believe his nerve. He was *sitting in the car right outside*. He never said a word to me when I announced where we were going, didn't try to talk me out of it or anything. OK, so I'm sure he wasn't expecting me to go into my friend's bedroom, but still . . . I ran outside and marched to my car, bawling my eyes out. The nightmare had finally come true. My dream man was no more. I took off my engagement ring, threw it at him, and told him if that was the life he wanted, go live it. He got out of the car, and I drove off.

That lasted about a month, and I forgave him *again* . . . oh, and we had another baby girl! Yes, I know . . . I can't believe I did that myself.

We decided it was time for a fresh start, and a move to a new place was what we thought we needed. Wanting to make things work, we moved to Durango, Colorado. We thought moving far away would fix everything. As you can guess, it did not. It was more of the same and even worse. I not only caught him stealing from me and my children, but doing drugs and drinking again.

That was the final straw! I sat him down and told him it was over, that I was done, that the kids and I would be moving back to Denver. *Multiple* panic attacks and continuous, nonstop anxiety began to plague me the moment I made that decision. I felt completely debilitated and also like the worst mom ever. Between the anxiety and my regrets, I could hardly function. It was time to reach out for support. I called my father and told him what was going on. In his love for me and his grandkids, he dropped everything immediately and drove the seven hours to Durango to help me. The next set of events that unfolded marked a low point in my life.

I was broke. I had spent all my money on the relocation to Durango. I now had to make hard decisions to raise cash, and the first decision was to sell *everything* I owned. This was an incredibly painful task —to sell things I had worked so hard for, for a fraction of their worth. I put an ad on Craigslist, and random strangers came and dug through piles of *all* my family's belongings, picking what they wanted and making (usually lowball) offers that in my desperation I had to accept. I heard my children begging me to keep their toys and watched them cry while I sold them. After selling my bed for mere dollars, I slept on the living room floor with my one-year-old daughter, snuggling with her and comforting her. Her drunk, belligerent father yelled at me while she watched. She was absolutely terrified by his rant, but I held her close and let her know it was going to be OK! Those were the same words that my father kept telling me. "It's going to be OK. You will come back from this."

I held onto those encouraging words from him throughout the move back to Denver . . . just my babies and me. Not long after returning, I received an amazing job offer and was able to get my own place. Eventually I bought furniture and started making our new home feel more and more like our space and refuge; our home. The more positive I started feeling about my life and where it was going, the more things began to turn around. I found a better place to live and arranged to rent it for six months. It wasn't long before the best opportunity manifested. I found a house that was a rent-to-own. Two years later, I was a homeowner. *I bought a house!* I did that . . . me! I did this all by myself, for my three kids and me!

I am so proud of myself for being brave enough to leave the man I thought loved me, but did not. I left with nothing, and rebuilt on my terms and with my resources. I was scared, my kids were scared. But now . . . it's over, and has been for six years . . . *I did it!* Plus, I fell madly in love with a man I met in July 2017, who I love more than I ever loved my ex-fiancé.

I can honestly say that I am profoundly grateful for having obstacles in my life that I was able to overcome. Those obstacles made me who I am today: a strong, independent woman, showing my kids I will *never* leave them, and I will *always* be here for them, no matter what. I have leaned into the career path of being a photographer who has a heart to give back. I long to serve those who have both visible and non-visible scars, who feel lost and alone. I am here to show them that they are *not* alone and to serve them on their new path of gratefulness and awareness.

**KNOW YOUR WORTH!**

CYNTHIA MORALES
Lake Wales, FL

# *A New Legacy*

I PROCRASTINATE. I've procrastinated sitting down and writing this story. I always procrastinate. I am a procrastinator. It's what I did—*up until now*, that is.

I wasn't sure how far back to take you on this journey. I'm going to look back to about ten years ago, when I completely lost who I thought I was. I lost the person I had worked so hard to build and become. By the time I reached my mid-thirties, this only child, latchkey kid, "me too" survivor, who grew up in New York City, raised by a single mom, had found success at levels that went against all the statistical proof of what was possible for someone like me.

With no college education and barely graduating high school, I worked my way up the corporate ladder and created a rewarding career in banking. I had a beautiful daughter, left an abusive relationship, and found myself a single mother working hard to create a life totally different from what I had experienced. I was earning six figures, was purchasing houses, was growing my retirement fund, was traveling, and was engaged to the man I believed was the love of my life. Then everything changed in what felt like the blink of an eye.

My stepfather died and my mother and siblings came to live with me and my fiancé, although they left after a year. I started experiencing serious health issues. I had already been dealing with mental illness, relationship issues, and financial difficulties. I experienced an actual mental breakdown, went bankrupt, and was betrayed by the man I was engaged to marry. I decided to move back to the small town in Florida my mom had taken me to, as a teenager. I had sworn to myself that I would *never* end up back there, but the Universe had other plans. I moved back, cashed out my retirement, and purchased a cottage with cash. I was determined to disappear, hide from the world . . . to make myself and my life as small as I possibly could. I had hit rock bottom and was living the life I had fought so hard to not make my reality. My new reality was food stamps, Medicaid, anxiety, depression, self-hatred, struggle, loneliness, and hopelessness. I had lost faith in not only in myself, but in God. My daughter was struggling, my mother was struggling, and I began to accept living that way as my fate, my karma.

In 2017, after a failed attempt at running a food truck business with my mom and sister, I found myself needing to get back into the workforce, and so I turned to the field in which I had found success in the past.

I got back into banking and hated it. In August of that year, I was introduced to a multi-leveling marketing company and had the opportunity to sell five-dollar jewelry. My best friend from high school, Chands, who lives in the same town as me, joined the company and although I found the idea insane, I was sure she'd be great at it. She is an extrovert, knows everyone in this small town, and loves hosting events. I had become the exact opposite: I had become introverted, avoided people, stopped celebrating life's milestones. My emotions were all over the place, my health appeared to be declining, and I'd convinced myself that there was no way I could find success again, and certainly not through some crazy multi-level marketing business opportunity.

I was in survival mode and although still struggling, I was beginning to rebuild my finances at least, so no way I was going to utilize my time or resources on such an absurd idea as five-dollar jewelry. Plus, Chands and I had just tried directly selling health products for one company and wine for another. Neither one of us was particularly healthy, nor did we drink wine; I have no clue what we were thinking, other than we just knew we were fed up with the lives we were living. Chands had done extremely well, just as I had expected, since she was an extrovert. Three months in, she again asked me to join the company, and although reluctant, I agreed to join in support of her. Three months after I came aboard, I attended a bootcamp for the business where I met and spoke with dozens of women from all walks of life, speaking passionately and joyfully about the success they had found with the company, and I experienced a total paradigm shift! I came home from that event, indulged in deep prayer and a conversation with God, and committed myself to really apply myself to my new venture for the next ninety days . . . and incredible things began to happen.

Time passed, and as we entered into 2021, I found huge success with that network marketing business, became a full-time entrepreneur, grew a team of over a thousand business partners, became somewhat of a social media influencer, and was making *more* money than I had ever made! I had survived the pandemic, started a second business, survived some very scary and heartbreaking situations with my daughter, and was beginning to see a light at the end of a dark tunnel!

I was so excited and thrilled by what I was accomplishing! I bought my first ever luxury car, moved into a luxury apartment while keeping the cottage to run my businesses and store inventory. I was traveling again, and best of all, in the spring, I learned I was going to be a grandmother! Financially, my situation was much better. My credit was much improved, and I even had some money in the bank . . . but in spite of my better circumstances, I couldn't stop feeling like a freaking imposter . . . *Who was I to be living such a promising life?*

Then, everything began falling apart. My health began declining again, money was slipping through my fingers, my relationship with my daughter had been devastatingly damaged, the industry I was in took a big hit, and folks were battling COVID-19 all around me. In spite of those facts, I managed to make it look like I was all good, on social media, as one does. On the surface, it appeared that I was living my best life. No one had any clue how chaotic my real life was and all that I was battling behind the scenes.

My bestie had given me the gift of a professional photo shoot for my business. I could barely pull myself together to get it done (remember, I'm a procrastinator). I booked the photo session for the very last day before the gift certificate expired. My anxiety was through the roof . . . I hastily threw some outfits together and did the shoot. I had no clue that this photo shoot would be the triggering factor for me to make some major changes in my life and my being. When the proofs from those photos hit my email, I didn't even recognize myself. I thought they were horrible. I shut down and then began spiraling out of control and heading straight into self-sabotage mode.

One day, as I was confiding in my best friend, Marla, about what I was going through mentally, emotionally, and physically, she mentioned that I should hire a life coach. *Huh? Who spends good money on stuff like that?* Plus, my businesses had just taken some major financial hits.

*I've already been through tons of therapy and counseling,* I thought.

*What in the world could a life coach do for me?* On the other hand, what did I have to lose? I would for sure lose my mind and all that I had rebuilt if I didn't try something different, so I began researching. What did a life coach even do? How would I find one? I stumbled upon a company called BARK and completed their inquiry form.

I was presented with several different life coach options, set appointments with a few and then came across "Laura Walker Coaching, LLC." Something about her pictures and bio immediately sparked my interest. She was the only one who met with me for an entire hour via Zoom as our introductory session. The others had their assistants contact me and only allowed an introductory call of 15–30 minutes.

I felt an immediate connection to Laura. I felt heard, seen, and authentically cared for by her, even though we had just met. I couldn't believe I was about to spend a substantial amount of money for her services in the midst of a total financial panic, but my intuition was telling me it would be worth the investment, so I signed up for her twelve-week Dream Builder program.

As we journeyed, my health improved, my relationship with my daughter improved, my depression faded, my outlook brightened, and my physical ailment fibromyalgia began to diminish. I was thrilled . . . I felt alive and full of passion and purpose for the first time in a long time.

As the holiday season of 2021 approached, my growth mentally and emotionally progressed to new heights! It was so exciting to watch God's abundance unfold around me mentally, physically, emotionally, and financially! Two weeks before Thanksgiving, Laura offered to host a Vision Board workshop for my direct sales team. Almost seventy people attended, tools were given, and a financial freedom mindset was taught. It was a great event that left my team inspired.

As December approached, I was notified by my landlord that

my rent would increase by $500 a month starting in January. I was definitely not in love with *that* idea. So, based on my new tools from coaching, and the support of friends and family, I entertained the idea of buying a house. I already owned a small cottage, but on January 21st, I received a mailer from "Redfin," a real estate brokerage and it was as if a lightning bolt had struck me! The idea of buying a house began to resonate inside of me very loudly. I began having dreams about owning a place to call home, a place to build a legacy for myself, my daughter, and my new grandbaby.

In February 2022, the house hunt began, and it was as if the vision of a beautiful home for my family was pulling me . . . it was all I could think about, night and day!

I toured new construction, but something about those homes wasn't resonating with me. I had always loved the charm and character of older vintage homes, like my cottage, so on January 21st, my house hunt officially shifted to homes with character that were already built.

And then my grandson was born on January 22nd. I fell head over heels in love and was so proud of my daughter, Ari, and the amazing mom she was being with baby Zaire.

Now I was even more driven to find a home for my growing family and build a legacy and beautiful life for us all. So the very next day, January 23rd, I called my Realtor and set up an appointment to see a house that had been featured in a marketing email. I was excited and hopeful that this was the house for us . . . but after a tour on the 24th, I knew it wasn't the right home for my family. It was lovely, but not for us.

After the tour, I gave feedback to my Realtor's assistant, whom I had just met for the first time. I explained that I needed a house big enough for my business to thrive, room for my daughter and grandson should they need to stay with me, and room for my mom when she visited from the Dominican Republic. The assistant, Erin, lit up. "Cynthia," she said, "we have this older house that we just listed and no one else has seen. I think it could be exactly what you're looking for."

We drove to the house. Every minute of the drive, I was internally thinking of reasons not to like the house. *It's too long a drive . . . it's too expensive.* Sabotage, sabotage, sabotage. I literally talked myself out of it before I even clapped eyes on it. Then I saw it. As I walked through the house, it felt *right*. It was roomy and had character. I tried to talk myself out of loving it, but no dice! I sent Laura a message asking if she thought I was crazy to be thinking about purchasing a house, and she responded, "Cynthia, do you love it?" In my heart, I already knew the answer.

On January 26th, I pulled the trigger and made an offer on that amazing house! It occurred to me that parts of the house reminded me of the vision board I had made earlier this month, it seemed surreal. Panic began to set in, and I asked God if I was making a mistake, because the first couple of houses I lived in had had a pool and this one didn't, but it was something I thought I would love to have. God responded, "Cynthia, a *pool??!!* I'll give you a whole *lake!*" This home was located directly on one of the only swimmable lakes in our area of Florida.

The next day, January 27th, my offer on the "lake house" was accepted. It's a day I will never forget . . . a dream come true. GOD is *amazing!*

After negotiations, inspections, repairs, and other things, I finally closed on the lake house on March 24th. After the closing, even though I had initially thought I would keep my cottage and rent it out, I started to feel the pull to let it go. On April 4th, I decided to sell my little cottage, visualizing an amazing family in it, loving it the way I had for so many years as I rebuilt my life. I began a twelve-week process of extensive remodeling to bring the cottage to a new level of beauty. It was a labor of love to make it wonderful for the next chapter in its journey.

By mid-June 2022, the cottage was finally ready for listing! My heart is so full. I love my new lake house and cannot wait for someone to make the cottage their home! The very first day, four showings were scheduled in the first twenty-four hours. Within five days of listing there were eight offers. We accepted an offer that scheduled closing within thirty days. The offer was $80,000 over the original estimate and $11,000 over the asking price.

Looking back on this entire sequence of events, I am in *awe*, just astounded at how events unfolded and provided amazing results and blessings for my family and me, simply because I listened to my heart and followed the vision God had given me. I was scared but I acted anyway, and now I have an amazing house on a lake, my family is with me, and I get to run my business out of my gorgeous lake house . . . all because I got in touch with a vision of what could be and faced my fear, walked in faith, and manifested God's abundance for me and my family, overcoming the obstacles and building a new legacy of success!

NIKKI GEORGE PAPADAKIS
Astoria, NY

## *The Courage to Decide*

I THOUGHT I would be married by now, with a few kids running around. Never in my life did I think I would still be single at thirty-two and starting over. Little did I know that *deciding* to start over would be the best decision I made in my adult life.

I got engaged to my longtime boyfriend the day before my thirty-second birthday. I thought this new chapter in my life would finally bring fulfillment as we embarked on this new journey together. Isn't this what girls are supposed to do? Grow up, receive a fairytale proposal, and get married to the man of our dreams? That's certainly what all Greek girls do! But boy, was I wrong! After my engagement, instead of excitement about what lay ahead, all I felt was fear and anxiety. I knew I had settled in my relationship, but thought maybe if I got engaged and started planning a wedding, maybe those feelings would change and I would feel differently.

Planning a wedding makes everything real. I realized that in a year my whole life would change, and with someone I wasn't sure I wanted to spend my life with.

I began to view marriage as a business partnership. I would

literally be signing a contract with my partner that would bind us legally to each other. So, I asked myself, the, *Would I go into business with this person? Is this someone who I can make decisions with? If we reach a disagreement, will we be able to compromise?* I imagined different scenarios in our life together, but my honest answer to each was always *no*. But how was I now going to get out of a relationship that'd I invested seven years in and still, I did not have a good enough foundation and understanding of who I was and what I wanted, to leave? Look at all the people I would disappoint, especially my family. Greek girls are raised to get married and have families. I couldn't find the courage to say, "This isn't working for me anymore and I think it would be best for us to break up." But I do believe that in our hardest times, God finds a way to save us.

As time went on, nothing changed. I was miserable for two months after our engagement. I reacted negatively to every conversation we had. We were having a lot of issues with venue and date discussions. We couldn't agree on anything. I derived no excitement or enjoyment from the planning; I just found it very stressful. All my initial joy was gone, and the wedding planning honestly just felt like a total burden.

We had a really bad argument one day. I think we were just fed up with the stress, and this particular day he cracked and told me he was done with me and wasn't going through with the wedding. I think God opened that door for me because He knew I couldn't do it myself. I could hear my inner voice telling me, "OK, Nikki, this may be the last opportunity you'll have to get out of this, so go through the door now that it's open." So, I did . . . and never in my life have I felt such relief. I was relieved it was over and that I didn't have to end it myself.

Three days later, my former fiancé came to see me and apologized for the things he had said, insisting that he hadn't meant them. I knew this was going to happen; it was our pattern. But during those three days I'd given a lot of thought to what I truly wanted and confirmed that he couldn't give it to me. This time things were different, and I had a strong resolve. So, I built up my courage and ended the relationship—for good! I was not going to settle for mediocrity when I know I am worthy of so much more.

After the breakup, I knew I needed guidance to find myself. That's when I found Laura. She has been coaching me in transformational principles for almost a year now. Through her support and guidance, my life has changed completely. Now at thirty-three years old, I am altogether a different person. I know who I am and what I want. I have a thriving career. I'm working out at the gym six days a week, which keeps my body fit and my mind clear. I created space to welcome love again and most importantly, I learned to love and put myself first in order to thrive in my next relationship.

I am so grateful for all I have learned and continue to learn about myself through this transformational journey. I thank God for every day I am able to wake up and be the best version of myself and continue to vibrate at a high frequency, attracting into my life people and activities that I love. I have never felt more alive than in this moment, and I am truly thankful for every minute of it.

JACK SMITH, JR.
Pittsburgh, PA

## *The Art of Charity*

AT ONE POINT IN MY LIFE, I was RICH. I was on top of the world, but felt empty inside. I was what is called a HENRY (high earner not rich yet).

I knew working eighty-plus hours a week was killing me, but I wanted more. Before long, this type of mindset would catch up with me.

My name is Jack Smith, Jr. I am a God-fearing man who places Him first in my life above anything or anyone else. I was born and raised in Pittsburgh, Pennsylvania and currently live twenty-five minutes east of Pittsburgh in a beautiful suburban neighborhood. I grew up with two brothers and one sister in a very strict, single parent household. As I got older, I realized that that was the best environment I could have been raised in to prepare me for my future. My mom was tough on us, but fair. She always encouraged us to try new things, have faith in God, and to always, always respect everyone.

I have been diligent about passing on those same qualities to my kids. I have three beautiful daughters: Tesia, Zaynah, and Iyonna. They are at the top of the list of my many blessings. We love getting out to do new and exciting things, anytime we can.

Most weekends, you can find us at a local park, an amusement park, or basically anything that involves a thrill! They keep me on my toes for sure.

I run several businesses that I started from the ground up. At the top of the list is my janitorial business that I started with a vision and dream in 2006 with only $500, one vacuum, and a driving obsession to make my name known in the cleaning world. My second business is an online store that I created in 2017 that sells solar products. I am a firm believer that fifty percent of the world's power will come from solar energy by 2050, so I wanted to make my mark in the solar world, in addition to the cleaning world. I also owned a frozen yogurt shop that opened in 2016 and closed in 2020. The shop offered fresh juices, over one hundred different toppings and eighteen different daily choices of the best frozen yogurt/ice cream/sorbet in the state. It was so successful; it drew local celebrities and politicians in to see what all the fuss was about! I worked hard to establish the shop as it was in a very busy, new strip mall. With the cost of the build-out, equipment and fees, I was left with $2.35 in the cash register to open the shop. Excited and *very* nervous, and with the help of my brother, Jerome, we opened the shop on November 12, 2016. It would be one of the best rides of my life!

In opening the yogurt shop, I had the honor of meeting a gentleman named Brett Malky, who has become one of my mentors. I have talked so much about this man that my friends tell me I have a man crush on him, and I'm totally fine with that! Although he downplays it, I constantly remind him how much of an impact he has had on my life and how grateful I am for him and his mentorship. Ironically, what brought us closer was some of my poor decision making, as well as finding out that we have the same religious beliefs. Along with Brett being successful, he is also a true family man!

Between operating those three businesses, I was an extremely busy person. My main source of income continued to come from my janitorial service. While a lot of money was coming in, even more was going out, leaving me with no income.

On March 15, 2020, my financial world started to crumble when I, along with millions of others, learned that there would be a global lockdown due to COVID-19. At the time of that announcement, I thought it was something that would pass in a few months or so—but that did not happen. I had no choice but to tell my employees that they would not be coming back to work. It was very painful to have these conversations, because I knew how much everyone, including myself, depended on having income security, and that was being taken away from us unexpectedly. I will never, ever forget some of the conversations I had with employees who had families, during which their hurt and confusion often turned into tears. It was the lowest point of being a business owner.

By 2021, two of my three businesses closed, eighty five percent of my income was gone, and all my credit cards were maxed out. I was down to a few hundred dollars to my name. I didn't know where to turn and felt the walls caving in on me. I felt stuck and became unmotivated and lazy. Any sense of direction on my life path was now lost. I was confused about how just a year earlier, I'd been living on top of the world, and now I was practically broke. Suddenly I found myself doubting every business move I had made.

I felt defeated. Since I grew up in poverty, my biggest fear was going back to being broke. Mentally, I shut down and couldn't get any forward motion going.

At that moment, I asked God to take over my situation and guide me through this rough time. I also asked him to use me by putting me in a position to help others . . . even though I was at the lowest point in my life.

Despite my prayers, nothing in my situation changed in the days that followed. In fact, from where I stood, it appeared to have gotten worse. My faith was being tried and torn apart.

One day, while sitting at a red light in my car, a homeless man approached the car with a sign that read, "Homeless Veteran. Can you help?" I normally don't have cash on me, but the night before I had made a withdrawal to give to my daughter for her first school book fair. I lowered my window and gave him the money without hesitation. That light didn't seem to change for ten minutes, as we had a good conversation about his family and his military service duties.

I drove off. When I returned to my house, I thought about the homeless gent's smile and the gratefulness he had exuded while we chatted. I recalled him repeatedly thanking me. It amazed me that a simple conversation could have that much impact on a person. What I didn't realize at the time was that our conversation had as much an impact on me as it had for him.

That day, the seed God planted in me to help others, even in my time of financial struggle, had now sprouted and was starting to grow rapidly! It prompted me to use my entrepreneur skills to found a nonprofit organization that I called The Art of Charity. The "soul" purpose of the organization was to support others, so they don't go through the same emptiness and helplessness I went through, when my world was falling apart. In our brief existence, we have formed partnerships with several local and nationwide foundations such as Walmart, The Tony Robbins Foundation, The Lisa Libraries, Hole Food Rescue, and others, to ensure assistance is available where it is needed.

A rich life consists fundamentally of being of service to others and has nothing to do with money, as I found out that amazing day. It is a lesson that I will hold deep in my heart and will continue to operate from, going forward into the days God blesses me with.

JANETTE WOLD
Rockwall, TX

## *Peace Keeping*

As I awoke every morning to the smell of coffee and cigarettes coming from the kitchen . . . I knew there would be just a few more hours of peace for myself, my very young siblings, and my dad.

Peace from the anger, rage, yelling, hitting, and cursing that would ensue as soon as my mom woke up from another all-nighter. Not the type of all-nighter you're probably thinking of, though. An all-nighter for my mom was staying up till 4AM, writing and rewriting long lists of endless chores for all of us to do the next day, sitting on the phone talking herself up to friends and family, researching another get-rich-quick scheme, lining everything up on paper towels so that nothing touched the counters, meditating, and lighting her last cigarette with the next one.

Ironically . . . she was never a drinker.

The smell of coffee and cigarettes together will always remind me of the "rage days."

Some nights if she was in a really bad raging space, she would rip us all out of bed to re-fold clothes, cut strings off the towels, or iron the sheets. All evening chores had to be done perfectly before we were able to go to bed, and if she found anything amiss after that, all hell broke loose. All laundry had to be washed daily. We had a towel load, a dark load, and a white load. We also had to shower only at night. We were never allowed to have a morning shower, because the shower had to be scrubbed nightly after "our filth" was washed off.

My mom always slept on the floor next to her bed so as not to dirty her bed, and every room in our house was blocked off except the kitchen, bathrooms, and bedrooms. We were allowed to sleep in our beds; however, we were not allowed to sit at the kitchen table to eat . . . only on the floor Indian style, and we could not rest our backs on the cupboards. The contents of our refrigerator consisted of Pepsi, salami, sweet pickles, squeeze butter, whole milk, and Melba toast. My mom rarely cooked, but if she did, she'd make a pot of chili or peas and macaroni. We were never allowed to eat breakfast because we would make a mess while she was sleeping.

My mother was massively OCD, germophobic, and narcissistic. She had a temper that would spiral in less than a split second. My dad and I were always trying to keep the peace, but we failed on many occasions. After pinning me in a corner and yelling at me, slapping and punching me, and calling me fat, she would miraculously and immediately forget about that and then say something like, "Honey, will you get me a Pepsi?" Although, oddly enough, she would always remember to write me a note for school excusing me from gym class so that no one would see all the bruising and lumps on my legs.

My safe zone was my bedroom, where I would go to lounge on my waterbed and read, talk to myself, daydream, or sometimes just cry. I loved my bedroom, and one day one of my older siblings (who had already moved out of the house) gave me a cassette player and a bunch of cassette tapes. Listening to music created so much healing and self-reflection for me . . . which I didn't realize at the time.

When I was in the eighth grade my entire body started to

change colors, I'd have huge patches of dry skin, and my skin would bleed and split! My mom said I had chicken pox, and after months of being covered from my neck down in a complete life-changing rash, she finally brought me to the doctor. I had a very bad breakout of psoriasis, which the doctor said was exacerbated due to stress! In hindsight, I understand!

My mom never allowed me to go to friends' houses, have friends over, or even take phone calls! I was also never able to go to any school dances or events, because the afternoon was when my mom would get all dressed up to go shopping and out to dinner without us. She was extremely self-absorbed and had not an ounce of self-awareness to know that her actions contributed to the destruction of my life. Clothing was scarce for me. I had one pair of 501 jeans, a pair of blue corduroy pants, and about five shirts, all hand-me-downs. When I entered high school, this lack of wardrobe was really hard to cope with. I had low self-esteem, and the bullying from classmates took a toll on me. My psoriasis had flared up again, and I had to resort to wearing the only long-sleeved shirt I had every day in an attempt to cover it up. Eventually the other kids noticed my skin condition, and the bullying became nonstop. Every part of my life was in disarray, which led to me rebel against everyone, including myself.

Interestingly enough, my mom didn't care about schooling, grades, absences, report cards, or community any more than she cared about sleeping or nutrition. If there was a family event, though . . . look out! We were the best dressed, best mannered, happiest damn family you could imagine! Our family pictures, holidays, and barbecues represented something way different from our reality. I longed for the life my cousins had and always wondered why we were cursed with such pain in our daily lives. As a kid, I often wondered if my aunts and uncles knew what was happening in our household. Years later, after I became an adult, I learned they *were* aware but chose not to get involved. Those events with family were much like being let out of a cage and being able to run free, only to be pulled back into captivity by your ankles. My mom hated all six of us, or at least that's what she told us on many occasions, and mostly we hated her, too . . . or maybe we hated the hate she had in her.

I took on the role of "mom" to my two younger sisters and did my best to protect them as they were growing up. I was determined to make sure that their experiences growing up in our dysfunctional home included some good "girl memories." We would play, laugh, and dance together, and I would sneak them food in their rooms.

My dad spent endless hours working to keep a roof over our heads and to support my mom's expensive taste. He was controlled by her, too, and had absolutely no power over anything she did. He would oftentimes just shake his head and agree with her. Whenever she went out of town, even for just a single night, my dad's whole persona would change and we would have big dinners, dance parties, or watch TV. He was a blast . . . when the thunderclouds were lifted.

After I graduated high school, we moved from Colorado to Arizona, which ended up changing the trajectory of my life. Up until that point, my self-esteem and confidence in myself was extremely low. I had no idea who I was and suffered badly from imposter syndrome.

My first job in Arizona was at a Mexican restaurant, where I met some amazing people who I still call friends today. While being the daughter of a narcissistic and abusive mom is and always will be an ongoing journey of growth, those first years in Arizona roused the longing for healing and prompted me to start my journey of self-discovery. I started a ritual that I call "Peacekeeping," where I would rise quite early in the morning to journal, read, plan my day, and drink my coffee. As in my childhood, this time of day has been ingrained in me to claim myself and my own peace.

I also found freedom from having a job, a car, new friends, and new surroundings where I could be anyone I wanted to be. A new me with a new story . . .

I soon started going to a therapist, and the most amazing words were said to me during one of the sessions. Those words stung me to my core, but then gave me a new perspective and a course to my path of healing. My therapist said, "It seems to me that you are looking for an apology from your mother. Please know that narcissists do not see what they are doing as wrong, and therefore will never apologize for their actions." Wow! Bam . . . right in the face! He was right! I was wanting my mom to wrap me in her arms, tell me she loved me, and acknowledge her aggressions. Now I knew that was never going to happen. I just needed permission to realize that truth, to pack my own proverbial parachute. So, I was on my own to seek out my own growth journey through friendships, laughter, boundaries, and boys.

By the time I was twenty-three, I had two beautiful daughters who lit up my world, and I vowed to make sure they heard the words "I love you" from me every day. Raising them has been such an honor in my life, and in some ways, they saved me by always, always loving me back. My girls are strong, confident, funny, and they know exactly who they are and how to love unconditionally. I am so very proud of who they have become and the paths they are taking as young adults today.

My ongoing healing has equipped me and led me into my passion of helping other women find peace within themselves through Mindset and Habit Coaching. I know now that my journey has not happened *to* me, it happened *for* me. It happened so that I can stand tall, be brave, and tell my story. Today, I work with amazing women who have so many different, but always compelling, life stories. I help them empower their lives and step into their highest self by stepping out of self-doubt, self-sabotage, and negative self-talk. My main goal is to help women take an overwhelmed and depleted mind, heart, and soul, and transform that into a clearer, curious, confident, and self-possessed space.

After all these years, I look back at my life knowing that I have found some true gifts through my "viaggio" ("journey" in Italian), which is now perfectly and unapologetically tattooed on my right arm. I release all the old patterning and pain that is not in alignment with my purpose in life. I will forever keep with me love, lessons, growth, and peace.

MATT ALEXANDER
Keller, TX

# *Making it Out of the Darkness*

As I sat waiting for my flight to depart, it hit me that this was the first trip I have taken in over two years. Life seemed normal again—bumper-to-bumper traffic, people congregating, and hurried travelers darting to and fro, to catch flights. I saw no social distancing nor signs directing people where to stand. The only remnants of the COVID-19 days were the face masks that kept the past present. Was the pandemic finally over? Was I dreaming?

Then, I started recalling how the past two years affected my life. The isolation, the horrific numbers, the fear, financial destruction, economic disaster, the darkness, health concerns and the uncertainty of the whole situation. Of *my* situation . . .

I'm Matt, and this is my story . . .

I grew up in a normal, middle-class family in the suburbs, a large, loving, Southern family who never had issues with money. We always had a home to live in . . . food to eat . . . a strong family bond. I always had a job and money in my accounts. I had a great credit score, and lenders wanted to give me more credit! Then the pandemic reared its ugly head.

In March of 2020, I was laid off from my longtime marketing job at a large healthcare organization. I quickly signed up for unemployment, thinking it would only be for a month or two, at the most. I started applying to positions, but there weren't many out there, at the time. So, that opened the door for me to concentrate on my side hustle—my own marketing company. I started picking up new clients and other short-term contract positions. Things seemed fine, and I was able to pay my bills. But, one month turned into two, then three, and before I knew it, my unemployment ran out. It was already eight months into the pandemic and I didn't have a full-time job. With no other options, I kept fighting and scraping to make ends meet.

Unfortunately, my efforts weren't enough. My credit cards were maxed out. My savings were depleted. Banks wouldn't lend me any money. I had to defer mortgage and credit card payments. My parents weren't able to help me, and my sisters were also experiencing similar situations. I was alone.

I applied to dozens of positions. I had numerous interviews. None resulted in a job offer. I was getting desperate and worried about having enough money for basics like milk and bread. For the first time in my life, I went to a local church for free groceries. I was so grateful, but also realized that time was running out. I was going through a deep depression that I had never experienced. I even started contemplating suicide . . .

One day, I received a message from a blond lady (her photo was included in the message) asking if I did email marketing. It was Laura Walker. I said absolutely! We met, and I began working for her company part-time. I found her positivity refreshing, and exactly what I needed. In hindsight, I know it was God who put us together.

Laura mentioned she had another company she was passionate about and invited me to a discovery session. I've never sought help for my problems, but at that juncture of my life, I desperately needed it. If anyone could help save me from my current situation, it was Laura. She helped me transform my thinking in no time at all! "Everything is made twice, first in the mind and second in action." I didn't really understand that in the beginning, but it became clearer as I did my exercises daily. I read my daily meditations to re-train my thoughts on money, vocation, and love. It wasn't easy by any means, but I kept going. Something in me said *this is going to work.*

Then, I started to see a shift . . . a big one. I decided to sell my home and move into an apartment in a complex I'd always loved; Mediterranean style and beautifully landscaped. If I was going to take a leap, that was where I wanted to land. So, I listed my house. In just two days I had twelve offers—all above asking price. The apartment had one unit left, and I got there just in time to secure it. If I'd waited even an hour longer, it would've been gone. It was all perfect timing! And the sale of my house gave me sufficient money to live on until the economy started opening up. I'd be able to survive.

Within a month, I received a call from a company needing full-time marketing assistance. I met with the owners, and they made me an offer on the spot. This wasn't just any job—it was the one I'd dreamt about securing, since meeting Laura. It was the perfect position for me. I couldn't believe it was finally happening! I couldn't have done it without the divine intervention of meeting Laura. I was finally me again, but better!

As the gate agent announced the boarding groups, I picked up my backpack and started smiling. I'd made it through the worst period in my life. The weight had lifted, and now I could enjoy life again. My credit cards are paid off, no household repairs to worry about, and a job I love going to every morning!

I finally made it out of the darkness . . .

DANI ATKINS
Kentwood, MI

## *The Unlearning of Unhappiness*

You know those personality tests that categorize and put an individual into a general box? The ones that lump everything about them into two to three dominant personality traits and voila! There you are! And yet it doesn't look or feel anything like that person? Have you ever taken one, and then immediately taken it again, hoping to get a more desirable result, purely because, surely you aren't so one-dimensional?

One night while attending a youth group student leadership meeting, I was sent to find a quiet place to sit, personality test and pencil in hand. I shrunk away onto the floor in a corner, hoping to become invisible. I knew what was going to happen. Predictions had already been vocalized by some of the group, and, to them, I was "easy, quiet, anxious, a loner." So whatever dull, most depressed category there was, I was certainly in it.

I felt embarrassed—there was no disguising the despair I constantly lived with. I felt judged and pitied. My inner critic was happy to chime in on the matter with a good ol' *They all probably feel sorry for you or are disgusted by you. Ooooh! Look at the sad girl sitting by herself! Are you going to cry, sad girl? Or write another depressing song about how sad you are? Pshh! Pathetic!*

I constantly felt my sadness taunting me about my depression, and particularly, in moments where I was socially judged and scored by a personality test. With very little confidence I was even doing it right, I completed it, tallied it up, and read my result. My inner critic laughed at it, but a deeper part of me felt unsatisfied; *surely, that's not really all there is to me.*

Years before, when I was eleven, I was told I had depression. My parents saw it in me, depression ran on my dad's side, and he had struggled with it his whole life. I remember the first conversation with him about it was like an out of body experience. The words were seared into my mind– that I was just not designed to be happy. That my DNA pre-determined that I would forever live miserably unless my body chemistry was artificially altered.

At first, my angsty, pubescent scoffed at the thought, but I couldn't ignore the similarities between my dad and I. The mood swings. The beyond-reason stubbornness and absolute feeling of betrayal when things didn't go my way. The sorrowful blue lens through which I viewed my life from underneath my own, personal, dark gray rain cloud. The *woe is me!* or *I'm such a loser* monologue that seemed to dominate my inner chatter. It sounded like him, but just in my own, personal, pre-teen way.

In hindsight, I know the objective of the conversation wasn't to permanently scar me, but to, in a strange way, encourage me. The depression wasn't my fault, after all. However, at that moment, at eleven years old, it enraged me. *How dare my own brain not be on my side! And how dare I subconsciously, reflexively deflect all the good and happiness that seemed to gravitate toward everyone else! And how dare my dad pass his stupid chemical imbalance to me?*

For years, it didn't even dawn on me to seek help, although

I desperately wanted and needed to have someone tell me I was actually okay. Having already decided not to become medicinally dependent to treat it and just find a way to deal, I didn't know what a therapist could do for me, beyond writing a prescription. I was furious about the idea of popping pills to feel happy, so I was bound and determined to try every other way before venturing that path, or just not worry about it at all. Again, a voice deep inside of me considered the matter, inspecting my unhappiness, and softly suggested that surely, this is not all there was to me.

Even though I *could* experience happiness, my default mode was feeling this all-consuming "darkness" well up inside me, from which there was seemingly no escape. Wherever I looked, I felt my depression was magnified, and I couldn't get away from it. Where I saw my siblings and peers connect and easily make bonds with those around them, I felt blocked. When people were making plans for their future studies at their dream colleges and jobs, I felt trapped in a haze of uncertainty. I become known for being sulky and withdrawn and disappearing at any given moment.

After living under that dark cloud for so many years, it became comfortable. It was easy to get upset and shut myself away from the world, for months at a time. My dark thoughts transformed from chaos to beautiful poetry in my eyes. (If Edgar Allen Poe could do it, why couldn't I?) I slipped into an eating disorder. I was addicted to emotionally and physically abusive relationships. I developed asthma. Because sadness was my fate, what did it all matter?

If it weren't for my interest in the performing arts and dance, I probably wouldn't be writing this today. My saving grace in high school was going to play rehearsals and getting out of my own head and into a different character's body for a few hours a week. And when I danced, it was magic—my spirit connected to something much bigger than my dark, insignificant fate. The world was shiny when I danced. *I* was shiny in those moments, too. Others saw me as shiny in my dance performances. And I followed that shiny road into a glamorous dance career.

In my early dance years, I enjoyed the performance aspect of the career and transferring my consciousness into a character, an alter-ego, that I pretended was the "me" without the dark cloud, that deserved love, that was valuable and had a great purpose in the world. She was the bright part of the poetry inside me, the comedy to my tragedy, the one who intimately knew peace and a life busting with sunshine. Outside of those shiny moments within my alter- ego, however, I was still the same girl struggling with her darkness. It permeated into my efforts at teaching and coaching—I always had my guard up and was afraid that people would see how pitiful I actually was, up close. Like every interaction was a question on a personality test that revealed more and more the sorrow I carried. So, even though I was good at dancing and really enjoyed it, my dance career (the majority of which, was teaching) crashed and burned.

I was thirty when I finally went to therapy, after my professional and romantic life took a dramatic turn, for the worse. I let go of the inhibitions about medicinal dependence—at that point I would have taken anything to release me from the grip of that constant chaos I felt swirling inside my brain. I had no idea where to begin, how much to reveal, what would be productive, but as soon as I sat in front of the therapist and was asked "Tell me a little about yourself and what you might be experiencing in life right now," the floodgates opened. The words poured out. And maybe it made sense, maybe it didn't. The therapist, Melissa, listened to me thoughtfully, diligently taking notes, nodding her curly head, offering an empathetic smile. After the torrential downpour of my life story, summarized in a quick fifteen minutes, she finally sat back and looked at me compassionately.

"You know, you've mentioned this dark, inner chatter a bit. I'm curious, whose voice is it you hear?" I thought about it. It was mine, but not really, and said so. She continued, "Often we think that since it's the voice in our head, that it is us, the true us. But, as you've just realized, that's not completely true. Fear can often have that voice, disguising itself as you. There's a primitive part of our brain that hasn't evolved yet and is triggered by fear, or what it perceives as dangerous, and it kicks in its narrative to keep us alive. But it's not you."

I hesitated. *What did that mean?*

"It means you're okay. You have a very active inner-chatter, but from what you told me, we can practice some calming techniques and positive exercises and see how you feel after a few sessions. What you're feeling is normal and we all have to deal with it at some point or another."

My jaw dropped.

"You mean I'm not hopelessly depressed? I don't need medication or dramatic forms of treatment to make it better?"

She smiled gently. "There's always hope! And no, we won't put you on medication, unless it's absolutely necessary. I think you're going to be perfectly fine without it."

I might have heard it before in a motivational meeting or read it in a book, but it never actually registered that it pertained to me and my situation. Not until my therapist told me directly.

Suddenly, my perspective began to shift. *I was actually, okay? And I could slow down the chatter by training my mind? That voice wasn't the real me?* I was familiar with the other side of me, the one that lived in a shiny world. *Was it possible that, that was the real me, just waiting to be realized?*

It wasn't a complete life overhaul from just that one session, but that first session began a massive gearshift in my life. I became obsessed with self-help books and TEDx talks about "one's mindset." I was starving for this information that I had longed to know, for over twenty years and consumed everything that reinforced this new idea: my genetic disposition didn't doom me to misery. I had a choice. I could *choose* to be happy. I started cleaning the lens through which I viewed my life and I leaned into the "shiny" side of me, and little by little, the blocks that hindered me from happiness began to dissolve, and the physical results in my life soon followed: I began teaching and coaching with confidence, gaining international attention in my industry for communication and outreach. I got certified in the highest level of the dance style in which I specialized, giving me the ability to travel around the world to coach, judge, and train other professional dancers.

I broke off a toxic relationship that had helped me nurture that dark cloud for years. I spent a summer exercising my newfound empowerment and designed a personal growth challenge to reprogram my victim mentality. I meditated. I invested time in the friendships that helped reinforce the new version of myself I was Be-coming. I went sky diving. I found myself in the healthiest romantic relationship I had ever dreamed of, all because I was led to the suggestion that maybe, just maybe, life could be different.

When I felt I had emotionally healed enough from the past to focus on the future, I got a life coach to begin truly discovering how big my world could truly be. I published a book, "No Cape Necessary," based on the personal growth challenge I developed, I published a journal, I learned to garden and paint, I manifested a trip to Iceland, I started volunteering and donating regularly, I began earning my certification in Pilates, and I discovered my world was vast and that so many things make me happy—life makes me happy—and I am not, in fact, an unhappy person. I choose the boxes I want to check, and no personality test can prove to me otherwise . . . I am a happy person, and I am completely enthused to embrace that truth daily.

MAUREEN CONNELLY
Willingham, DE

## *My Life as a Nurse*

A BEAUTIFUL FALL DAY IN 1972. Clear blue skies, a slight wind, and excitement in the air. Today will change my life forever, for today, is my first day of nursing school. As a young girl, I had dreams of becoming a surgeon. I didn't want to sit behind a desk working nine to five; I wanted to make a difference in people's lives!

My parents were always supportive of my ambitions until the time that is branded in my memory for life. One day, my dad sat down with me and we talked about my future. He wanted to discuss my goals and dreams. *Why is he doing this again?* I wondered. Once again, I explained to him that I wanted to go to college, to medical school, then an internship and residency program, and then I would become a surgeon. He smiled and said, "How are you going to pay for all that?"

His response stunned me. You see, I assumed my parents would be undertaking the costs of my education. To my surprise, Dad told me, "Maureen, I'm sorry, but your mom and I cannot afford this! You'll have to get a job!"

I was upset and deeply disappointed. I always believed my parents would help me. Now with this new intel, money was a big obstacle and getting a job was out of the question. I needed to utilize my time for study. I had always been an average student with questionable study skills, I could learn different things, but retaining what I learned was a different story. I soon decided I would have to settle and become a nurse. It would be a much shorter time in school and not nearly as expensive as medical school, and hopefully I could accomplish it . . .

I was excited to begin classes. I saw the excitement on the faces of my fellow students and made new friends. The first class we were enrolled in was the "Fundamentals of nursing." In that class we learned basic nursing knowledge, such as taking vital signs: not just body temperature, but blood pressure, pulse and respiratory rates, and being able to recognize abnormalities. We also learned how to make hospital beds properly. Our first clinical assignment was to make six hospital beds using correct techniques and be finished within thirty minutes or have a good reason why we couldn't get it done. When I entered the room where I was assigned to change the beds, I introduced myself to the patients. Sitting in their beds before me were six handsome young men. I was so excited at the sight of them. Could I possibly flirt and do my work simultaneously?! *Yes, I can do this,* I told myself with a smile. We chatted and got to know each other, there may or may not have been a little flirting going on.

I checked the time and to my horror saw that I had only five minutes to complete my assignment. That put me in a state of panic, with six beds to make in five minutes. Obliviously, too much chatting and flirting had gone on! How was I ever going to complete this assignment? The men saw how anxious I was, and three of them offered to help me. They informed me they were only in the hospital for routine testing and were healthy enough to assist. Even better, they were members of the Delaware National Guard and were already familiar with making beds. What a lucky girl I was!

I soon learned that the instructor was running about five minutes behind schedule. That extra few minutes helped me complete my task. The instructor arrived at my assigned room and rang saying it was time to be graded on the assignment. After completing the inspection, the instructor said to me, "Good job, Maureen!" That was my first successful teamwork exercise, and its successful outcome left me giddy with excitement!

We were also required to take the patients' vital signs and notate any deviation from the norm. That part of the assignment went without a hitch. I was so excited to have done well—of course, with a little help from my six handsome friends.

Taking tests is not one of my strengths. I could study for a week ahead of a test, know all the info the day of the test, but somehow my mind always seemed to go blank when I needed it most —*during* the test!

I truly had underdeveloped study habits, and in retrospect, what did I think I was going to retain? Sometimes I felt as if the medical books for nursing instruction were written in a different language. Of course, they were in English, but it took me quite a while to comprehend all the information they held! I lacked self-confidence, very rarely did I hear the nuns in the Catholic school I attended say, "Nice job" or, "I see you're having difficulty with this subject. How can I help you?" Complimenting students or offering to help them were things that seldom occurred. We did have study groups, but those groups had their own issues and sometimes were more of a hindrance than a help. However, we did help each other as much as we could.

My first year of nursing school was amazing, but extremely hard. I was so mesmerized by the function of the body. I often thought, *how will I ever remember all of this?* I was able to learn, but *retaining* the knowledge was a different story.

Nursing school was a fountain of learning. We had reading

assignments, clinical assignments, and, of course, visual assignments. These movies were on topics we had been taught by the instructors for review. A life-size skeleton was used for teaching anatomy and for presentations by groups and individuals. One afternoon, our instructor informed us that she had to attend a meeting for approximately one-and-a-half hours. She instructed us to use our time wisely. That certainly was one of the worst things she could say to a class of immature eighteen-year-old girls. We became bored easily, so the search was on, to see what we could do to entertain ourselves. It was a cold winter day, and our group decided to dress our skeleton—whom we had named Oscar—as if he was going outside in the cold winter weather. We gave him a hat, scarf, gloves, and someone put an unlit cigarette in his mouth (in those days we all smoked cigarettes, which were easily accessible). Upon completion, our class was very pleased with our handiwork. We had used our time wisely—or so we thought—and Oscar looked so cool!

Our instructor returned from her meeting and was absolutely speechless upon seeing what we'd done to Oscar. She was furious and demanded to know why we did that. We reminded her that she'd told us to use our time wisely, adding that we were trying to get along with the skeleton. But someone made the mistake of telling the instructor that we were bored! She went on a rant for at least fifteen minutes telling us how immature we were! "Don't you know how much the skeleton cost?" she chided. "Don't you know what would happen if it needed to be replaced?" She was so angry that she dismissed us early . . . and she made sure we could never again say we were bored in her class.

As we entered our second year of school assignments, our projects—*and* our patients—became more complex. We were given exams, exams, and more exams, group projects, and the hardest part of all—clinical rotations. Our instructor was by no means warm and fuzzy. I was so afraid of her because I couldn't figure out how to read her! When she gave an assignment, it had better be executed exactly as directed, or you certainly would pay the price for not following directions.

The patients we were assigned were quite complex cases, and as their nurses, we needed to be familiar with their diagnoses and medications they were taking. We were responsible for knowing the reason each medication was assigned to our patients, the dosage, and any potential side effects. This assignment put me in panic mode, first because of the depth of it. Second, I perceived myself to be a poor student, and third, I wanted to avoid the wrath of the instructor if I couldn't answer one of the questions.

The most challenging part of the year was the exams given by the National League of Nursing (NLN). These tests were supposedly a predictor of how each student would do on the state board.

*Another test for me to fail*, I thought. How could I possibly do better than I predicted and perceived myself to be? I went ahead with the exams and did my best, and several weeks later I received a call from our warm and fuzzy instructor. She asked to see me in the office. It was never a good sign to get a call like that, based on my experience. I was so nervous to receive the news that awaited me . . .

My heart sank as my instructor explained that I did extremely poorly on the NLN exams. She stated that if I did not get tutored in preparation for the boards, I would never pass. She also went on to say she did not think I could become a nurse because I seemed to lack the intelligence it required (a nice way of saying I was just plain stupid). She then went on to suggest that I might want to consider another profession. Many times, throughout the conversation she implied that I was stupid. It astounded me that a teacher would say such things to a student. This was by no means encouraging or flattering. It set the tone for how things would move forward, for me. So I resolved to work harder to prove her wrong.

Senior year came and went with much anticipation for things

to come. We were becoming graduates of nursing school, taking state boards, and finding jobs. Being a graduate nurse was like being in first grade again. You always have someone looking over your shoulder and have to perform tasks three or four times with supervision, before you are permitted to do it on your own.

I overcame my self-limiting beliefs about testing and became a seasoned nurse with an illustrious career. After forty-two years of serving as a nurse, I retired and now tutor up-and-coming nurses who maybe have the same fears I did so long ago. Do I regret being a nurse? Absolutely not! Once a nurse, always a nurse. I have made lifelong friends, learned a wealth of information, and worked with amazing people.

In closing, I want to stress that the only one responsible for your happiness is you! Do not let anyone tell you that you're not smart enough. Take steps of faith on your way, even if it's a possibility you don't want to explore. *You will never know what you are capable of until you try.*

I have worn many hats during my nursing career. I am an educator, a troubleshooter, a manager, and most of all, a loving independent woman. This did not come easy. There were lots of ups and downs and lots of tears along the way, but also lots of laughter! Reflecting on nursing school, all I could think of was what the instructor had repeatedly told me, that I wasn't smart enough to become a nurse. From that experience, I made up my own mind to never treat anyone the way that instructor treated me. I would never hurt anyone with such cruel words. I felt as though I had to prove that instructor wrong, that I *could* become a nurse. In a way, I thank her for sparking my determination and drive to succeed. However, in reality, I only needed to prove to *myself* that I did my job well; that was all that truly mattered.

SVETLANA FARWELL
Hurst, TX

## *The Angel's Hand*

I MUST HAVE HAD an angel's hand on my shoulder growing up.

When I was a kid, I used to dream a lot. Who doesn't, right? I dreamt of being a princess in a big white castle, where I would have a HUGE room filled with floor-to-ceiling white shelves, each filled with some type of . . . fruit.

Before you raise your eyebrows, I can explain! Growing up, my family lived in a VERY remote and very cold part of Russia, and fresh produce was a rare and expensive treat. What a joy it was for that little girl to lay in bed every night, dreaming of every imaginable fruit and berry she could have, as much as her little heart desired, in a beautiful room that she did not even know could exist! We did not have the concept of walk-in closets or pantries at the time.

To this day, some, ahem thirty-five years later, it still makes me smile.

Call it fate, God, karma, divine intervention, but one HAS to believe in a higher power. I must—when I look back at the incredible events that unfolded over the course of my life and took me further than I knew to think of or dream, at the time.

Back where I am from, you had to "know someone" to go

places. To get ahead. Even to get things others take for granted. My family didn't. My parents were a blue-collar, hard-working, but always struggling couple. They raised my brother and I, gave us everything they could: education, a roof over our heads, food on our table. But they did not have the clout, they weren't "in the know." They never made it into those higher circles of the local society. So, it had to have been a MIRACLE, that a greater, higher power took me under its wing and gently carried me along my journey.

When I was in middle school, we were to sign up for a foreign language course as part of the curriculum. There were only two choices, English and German. I happened to attend the information session for the English class—and fell in LOVE with it, from its first sound. When I came home and told my parents, they said no. My parents (my mom, really) explained that they studied German in school, and my older brother also took German, so if I chose English, they would not be able to help me with my homework, therefore it would not be practical for me to take that path.

To be a good, obedient daughter, I went back the next day to change my class. But as FATE would have it, the German teacher had unexpectedly quit, and English became the only language option. I couldn't get enough of it; I loved English.

I will never know all the sacrifices my parents made to support me. It warms my heart now, that I am a parent myself, to think back and understand how difficult it must've been. Mom sought out extra courses that I could take after school or on the weekends; I had to take public transportation by myself and walk the city streets at night, to get to and from those classes, but it all seemed worth it, somehow.

Then my parents saw an ad in the paper about open spots in a prestigious target school, with emphasis on English as a foreign language and signed me up. Before I knew it, I was a part of the very first group of students from my city to go to the USA—an unthinkable, unimaginable honor and privilege that few could even fathom to dream of. I returned from that trip, my face muscles sore from SMILING the entire time there, infatuated even more with what was yet an unknown entity to me, but what would eventually become my future home and the birthplace of my five beautiful children.

When we were graduating high school, a friend of mine talked me into going away for college with her. The university she (or rather, her dad) had in mind was offering a prestigious degree in oriental languages, which was highly valued in the part of the country we were in, but required overcoming intense competition through several entrance exams, one of them being in English.

I was good at it, and my friend was eyeing my services as a free tutor to help her beat the odds. While my English was pretty good, I knew nothing about oriental countries or their culture. But somehow, I went along with my friend's plan. We both got in.

Three years into studying the Korean language, while still minoring in English, it happened, I JUST happened to walk through a different part of my campus, where the English majors, were studying. I saw a flier about a contest for a one-year, all expenses paid, scholarship to a US college. All I had to do was win against a few thousand hopefuls taking a Test of English As a Foreign Language (TOEFL). No big deal. The TOEFL was known to be a grueling, demanding, highly technical, and a multi-hour grammar and vocabulary testing ordeal. After completing those components, we would be tasked with writing a hopefully overwhelmingly, impressive essay in a foreign language. Finally, we would have an in-person interview that must be aced.

Nobody was around to explain to me just how slim my chances of success were, so I signed up. And I won. In a city of over seven hundred thousand, I was one of only two victors of that incredible opportunity.

But wait, there was one little problem. I DID NOT KNOW I had won. We did not own a computer or a cell phone, not even a landline. It was summer, and all students were out on a break. It just so happened that I had left my English dictionary on campus, so I called my dean from a pay phone while being out and about . . . "What are you still doing here??" she cried excitedly. "You won the contest!!" You could have knocked me over with a feather. "But you must hurry, you need a passport, and the paperwork must be completed, and you have to be on a plane by . . ."

You would have to scroll back up to the beginning, where I said this wasn't supposed to happen to people like me and my parents. People like us, with no money, no pedigrees, no connections, we didn't get chances like this. This couldn't be happening. But it was.

I went on that academic scholarship. I studied hard, I worked on and off campus, I traveled, I made friends. I also fell in love with a ridiculously handsome young man, my future ex-husband of thirteen years and the father of those five kids. It was love at first sight, on my birthday, of all days, September 25, there was a floor meeting in our dormitory about the rules and regulations and expected behaviors of students and what not. He was sitting on the floor across the room, and he laughed at my broken English joke and the rest was history.

*Up Until Now*, it was unbelievable to think that first of all, I would give birth to five children, me?! Second, that all five of them would be born and raised in Texas, USA. That was not in ANY part of those princess dreams growing up, nor could I possibly know to dream that grand, aim that high, hope that freely.

But I did get that walk-in pantry. Though I now keep my produce in a more practical crisper compartment of the stainless-steel side-by-side Samsung refrigerator, a South Korean brand, you see, as a nod to my college major.

## SCOTT & TIFFANY FINKELSTEIN
Keller, TX

# *The Best is Yet to Come*

AUGUST 6, 2010. Tiffany and I will never forget that date. That is the day my wife and children delivered me to the Federal Correctional Institution in Forrest City, Arkansas.

This was not how things were supposed to go for me. But I had made some poor choices, some *really* poor choices, and now I found myself convicted of wire fraud. The sentence? Eighteen months in prison. I was scared to death.

At the time, Tiffany and I had been married a little over six years. I will never forget the first day I saw her. It happened several years earlier. I was sitting outside my place of employment when I saw this gorgeous, tall woman in a beautiful green dress striding smoothly across the parking lot. I knew at that very moment . . . I would marry her.

Now, six years later, with a string of poor decisions hanging over my head like a black cloud, I thought for sure this would break up my wonderful family, that I'd lose them forever. Tiffany most certainly was going to leave me. She definitely had just cause to do so.

Even though I was going "away" for a while, I had built a lucrative printing service with a business partner. He had graciously agreed to take care of my family for the duration of my eighteen-month absence. It was a huge relief to know that during the time I would be "away," things would remain economically stable for my beautiful wife and our five kids.

Unfortunately, agreements are not always honored. I was in prison and there was very little I could do to try to make things right for my family. In less than a few months of my incarceration, my business partner had stopped making the agreed upon payments of $12,000 a month to support my family. It was awful knowing I had no way to help my family with the financial crisis I had left them in, by getting locked up. Dealing with the fact that I created this situation was an even harder pill to swallow . . . I was devastated.

Sadly, my wife and kids were forced to leave our house and move in with her parents while I was incarcerated. Dealing with the fact that she had five young children to support and a husband in prison, Tiffany began searching for a job to keep food on the table and things in forward motion for our family. She eventually found a job and kept the family intact. And what's more, she didn't leave me, as I expected she would. She showed her true strength and courage during this time, and I love her very much for her grit and determination.

She moved our family into a cheap, rundown apartment near the Texas Christian University (TCU) area of Fort Worth, Texas, and that was the "home" I went to upon my release. It was not the type of place we were accustomed to. The roaches were so big you could put a saddle on them.

When I was released from the halfway house, I returned to what I knew and tried to get a job in printing again. All ties were cut with my previous business partner and all rights to that business were now forfeited. Corporate America would not have anything to do with me for a minimum of seven years until the history of my incarceration fell off my public record. So, I bit the bullet and did what I could with what I had to support my family. My first job felt like a slap in the face. I was making $300 a week making phone calls in an office. Not only was it humbling, but it didn't pay the bills, so I left that job and went to work for a roofing company.

Then, that spring, the clouds finally parted, and the sun began to shine on my family again. A Texas spring hailstorm hit, and with the resultant repair work needed to people's roofs, we were in the "chips" again. Grateful for the divine turn of events, we found a house to rent in Keller, Texas, and our lives started improving drastically. Within a couple years, I went to work for "Next Door Painting," a painting service in the Dallas/Fort Worth area. I began to build a territory and add members to my team. I could feel the life coming back into me. The future was looking up for my family and me. I have never looked back!

Every year has gotten better. Then I met Laura Walker. She was a guest visitor at a meeting of a professional networking group that I had belonged to for several years. I knew immediately that I wanted to connect and work with her to take my success to the next level, both personally and professionally. I wanted to build a deeper bond with my kids, as well as a legacy so we would never have to endure financial hardships again. Laura and I journeyed together through coaching. With her support, I became president of "Next Door Painting" and have realized the financial potential that had eluded me, since my release from prison. With my promotion to company president, I received a significant raise and bonus plan. I have a team of nine sales managers under me now and love the work I do.

My marriage is stronger now than it has ever been. My relationship with my children is evolving and getting stronger day by day. My time in prison and its immediate aftermath was the worst period of our lives, a truly dark time. I never thought we would make it through, but we persevered, and Tiffany was the glue that kept us together. I'm forever grateful for her and her commitment to me and our family. I can't help but feel, though, that the best is yet to come!

HANNAH KERSEY
Dallas, TX

## *Onward and Upward*

WRITING THIS STORY has been hard for me. It was a challenge to sit down and even *think* about writing this story. I didn't know where to start. A turning point? Hell, I could think of five, ten, twelve turning points in my life. An epiphany? I have epiphanies all the time. Maybe not life-altering ones, but I frequently experience the "young woman navigating life on her own" type. I guess my struggle has been that I thought I was going to write about how I ended up doing an attempted hike of the Appalachian Trail. That's a good story, and it represented a turning point in my life. Lots of big changes and big emotions, but it's something we've all heard before: "Twenty-four-year-old woman feels lost and confused in life, decides she needs a change and will start living for herself blah, blah, blah" . . . you get the picture. However, the more I sit here and type, the more I realize that the story I'd like to tell began on the trail, not before. Specifically, it starts at Bly Gap, mile 78.2 of the Appalachian Trail . . .

The rain slaps my face and legs like little needles pricking my skin over and over. It's been raining like this for hours. I lower my head to keep the rain off my face as much as possible. It's fucking freezing. This was my first time hiking in weather like this. Thirty-seven degrees out, and I'm soaked to the bone. I remind myself that just a mile back I crossed over from Georgia to North Carolina, an accomplishment to be proud of.

Getting through Georgia was hard. I didn't have any sort of trail legs or real hiking experience, and here I am, climbing mountains every day. But it's just under three miles to the next shelter, where I can stop for lunch and get out of the rain, even if it's just for thirty minutes.

As I hike out of Bly Gap, the trail begins to incline. Normally I'd curse and be annoyed because inclines mean burning legs and shortness of breath, but today I'm happy. Today an incline means heat . . . I'll generate more body heat, which my rain jacket will keep in, nicely. My joy lasts about four-tenths of a mile, when I realize that what I thought was the top of the incline is only a plateau. I have an even steeper climb in front of me.

The wind is picking up, the gusts so strong they almost knock me down. The rain turns to a drizzle, which I'd be thankful for had a thick wall of fog not rolled in, making it almost impossible to see my own hand in front of my face. I've never felt so alone on a trail before. Even when hiking by myself for the day, I would pass people or stop for lunch on a nice rock next to some other hikers. But today is different. I haven't seen one person all day, and that realization slowly sinks in. As I hike up the incline, I become more anxious.

My anxiety grows with every foot in elevation I gain. *Am I going the right way? I don't even know anymore. I can't see jack shit in this fog. What if I get blown off the side of this damn mountain? I should just turn around.* Then I start doubting myself: *And do what, hike five miles back to where I camped before? Dammit, Hannah! If you were in better shape, you would have been moving faster and would have gotten to the shelter by now. You're so fat; how did you ever think you could do this?* I stop. The weather terrifies me, but I'm even more terrified of myself.

My thoughts, originally coming from a place of injury and safety, turn to self-doubt just like *that!* I stand, scared and alone, thinking for a long time. So long it's almost as though the weather around me has stopped completely. I think about the horrible way I speak to myself, how I would never say the things I say to myself to my enemies, so why do I say them to myself? I'm supposed to love myself . . . right?

A gust of wind nearly blows me down, waking me from my inner turmoil. In an instant, my mind returns to the trail. The rain has started again, and it's coming down hard. That's when I understand: The only way to get out of this situation, both physically and mentally, is to keep hiking, onward and upward.

The next two miles fly by. Something has changed; I realize no one is coming to save me. No one is coming up behind me to make me feel less alone, or to give me a hug, or to tell me to be nice to myself, or to tell me that I can finish the climb. The only person who can do that is me. I have to be there for myself.

Arriving at the shelter is the biggest sigh of relief I have felt thus far in my journey. Seeing the smiling faces of people I had camped with the night before huddling together against the three wooden walls of the shelter is the best greeting I could ask for. Dropping my pack, I say, "So I guess we're not making it another five miles today, eh?" They all laugh and agree we've had enough for the day.

Another through-hiker named Cricket, who I met the day before, has saved a spot for me in the shelter, so I don't have to set up my camp in the rain. It's a remarkably kind gesture from a new acquaintance, so kind that I cry. The Trail works in mysterious ways.

We all ate, sharing interesting facts about our day's hikes, and I begin to realize it's been a physically and mentally challenging day for everyone. The people I've compared myself to are also fighting inner battles and conquering own mental mountains, just like me.

The temperature dips to twenty degrees that night, and the next morning we find our wet clothes frozen to the line, the mud from the day before slippery with ice, yet we all get dressed, put on our packs, and hike on. On to the river and on to the next mountain . . . Standing Indian Mountain, to be exact.

I'm nervous about this mountain; the climb up looks intense on the Trail App on my phone, and my muscles are sore and stiff from the cold and rain the day before. As I begin the climb, I realize the incline is actually pretty gradual, at least compared to the day before. The sun beams down on my face, and I'm thankful.

I find myself thankful for the sun and thankful for the birds chirping. I find myself thankful for my arms and my legs and how far they have carried me. And I begin to realize that I'm capable of so much more than I ever thought. I've walked almost a hundred miles, for Christ's sake. This body has carried me almost one hundred miles. *Wow!* As I reach the summit of Standing Indian Mountain, I realize I have just hiked uphill for two miles. I hear music playing as I approach the summit and see another hiker sitting playing guitar and singing. I go to stand beside him on the top of this mountain and look out at the valley and peaks I have hiked in the days leading up to this moment. I see lakes and towns and see how hard my body has worked to get me here. A mountaintop is not a place you can drive to; you must work to get here. I'm overcome with emotion, tears streaming down my face. The other hiker stops playing and asks me what's wrong, and I tell him my tears aren't from sadness, but from happiness. I tell him that have just realized that I haven't believed in myself for a long time, and that as I stand here, looking at all I've accomplished, I now not only do I *believe* I am capable, I *know* I am.

I hiked for another week before learning that two of my grandparents had become ill, at which time I made the decision to go home. Going home was hard. Adjusting to life in the city after thirty-five days of sleeping in the woods was difficult, on top of the deaths of my Grams and a close coworker and friend.

I felt I didn't know how to be in the real world and began to fall back into self-doubt and anxiety. The negative self-talk slipped back in, almost as though it had never left. I was sitting in my car after my Grams' funerals, feeling overwhelmed and lost. *What was I supposed to be doing?* I wasn't supposed to be back for five more months, but here I was, in my car outside my apartment, back to the life I thought I had left. I screamed and cried, and then it all came flooding back to me. The feeling of being alone on the mountain in the pouring rain. The fear I felt then and the fear I currently felt. I reminded myself that I am capable, strong, and a damn badass. I am twenty-four years old. I'm not going to have it all figured out. I mean, do any of us? But as I sit here typing this story, I do know that I believe in myself, and that the only way to leave where I am and get to where I want to be, is to keep hiking—onward and upward!

PHILIP KERSEY
Keller, TX

## *Finding Me*

I HAD BEEN STRUGGLING for a long time with friends, family, work, and myself. At my job, being a hardworking employee, I began to find fault with my coworkers: they displayed chronic laziness, apathy, and favoritism because of gender, among other observations (judgmental much?) My pattern of thinking trapped me in a constant state of disappointment. This filter resulted in my projecting how I felt about myself, onto other people. It created a struggle to have respect for others; I had to force myself to forget about whatever it was I saw flawed about them. Sometimes this forgetting came too late; the self-sabotaging was already in full force.

Twenty-two years old, with a rebel streak a mile long, I was trying to put my life together. My biggest obstacle was . . . *me!* I began college in the small Texas town where I had been born. My goal was to become a Licensed vocational nurse (LVN). With the help of financial aid and my grandparents, I eventually moved into my own apartment. This was the first place of my very own. I was so proud of it. Life was really looking up and I was enjoying the journey . . . but it didn't last long.

A friend, who I had known for several years, called me and told me she was about to become homeless and needed a place to stay. Being someone who always felt misunderstood, I always put a lot of effort into understanding others, even to my detriment. Well, my friend moved in, and my home life quickly became a struggle. Not knowing how to set boundaries, I lost all sense of control. I would react with anger internally and unseen and would never speak out about how I felt. Two struggles were going on inside of me. On one hand, I wanted to tell my friend how I felt, and on the other, I harbored the fear of making her uncomfortable or mad. So instead, I suffered in silence and never spoke up. This pattern led me to feel as if I was trapped in my own apartment with no control whatsoever.

I ended this uncomfortable roommate situation by running away. It was a user relationship, and I didn't have the tools to set boundaries in my *own* apartment. One day, at the end of my rope, I rolled up some weed into a blunt, got into my truck, and went for a drive to the country to escape. I didn't want to go back to the apartment, but I didn't have anywhere else to go. Then, like magic, I got a phone call from an old friend. Hindsight usually being 20/20, it probably was meant to happen this way. She invited me to visit her and her family, whom I loved dearly, and they loved me back! Her mother had been there for me through so many of my hard times and accepted me, no matter where I was in life. To this day I am still growing my hair so it can be as long as hers!

I didn't go back to my apartment. I left with a few belongings . . . I really didn't have much so that was easy. I stayed at the house of my friend's family for the next three days, ignoring my roommate's texts. On the morning of the third day, we went to a mutual friend's house to hang out and catch up. We were pulling into the driveway upon our return when my friend's little brother came running out of the house, screaming, *"Mom's dead!"*

Needless to say, it was a very difficult next few months. My friend, at twenty-two the same age as me, her twenty-six-year-old brother, little brother and little sister, eighteen years old, all lived with their mom. Their father had been stationed in Afghanistan for the last ten years and came back periodically. When he returned home after his wife's passing, we discussed my staying with them to help with the youngest sister, who was born with kidney disease and required constant medical attention. Between working in the medical field and my to school to become an LVN, I knew enough to do everything required. It was a perfect arrangement: I needed a place to live and they needed support.

I returned to my apartment, and after getting my belongings, I left and never looked back. I became a live-in caretaker for my friend's sister, after her mother's death. Little did I know I would soon be given housekeeper duties as well. But with no self-respect and no tools to create boundaries, I soon was left with nothing but taking care of this family in the midst of their grief, day in and day out, without time to care for myself.

This arrangement lasted for two full years. Soon after the funeral, I began taking my "patient" to dialysis three days a week, which was a forty-five-minute drive each way. While helping her maintain a healthcare schedule and keeping her room clean and neat, I also did laundry and picked up around the house. Because I didn't know my worth or how to set healthy boundaries at the time, I never asked for any pay. In fact, my filter of the world was so distorted that it didn't allow for any self-respect and the corresponding actions to support myself. I would go above and beyond, doing the most, to ensure a roof over my head, to my own detriment.

Slowly but surely, I became resentful of the situation. But I knew I'd done it to myself, and I was mad at myself for allowing things to play out this way. I was busting my ass to have a place to live, but in the process not having time to work a job that could support me outside of living with them. The worst part about this cycle I was in was, that I felt trapped. I felt unable to support and even care for myself, because the filter told me *you're only here if you do what they want . . . if you disappoint them, it will endanger your very safety and security*. I had been homeless a few times before, and I knew I didn't ever want to find myself in that position again.

After two years, one night I laid in bed, reflecting on all that had happened, feeling desperate and distraught. I realized that only I could be responsible for my self-respect. It was a serious wake-up call . . . one that I answered.

Self-respect is something I was not used to acting on in my life. I had few impulses at this point that were healthy. Usually, these impulses played out in the form of overcompensating to keep people around or to make myself look better than I felt inside: *Hey, look at me! I'm* worth *keeping around!* So, the prospect of me doing something for myself that required me to relinquish my "social security" blankets, took massive amounts of self-reflection and knowing my feelings. In hindsight, that one moment of clarity revealed the need for change in how I navigated my life. I needed a new filter. But at that moment, all I knew was that what I had been doing wasn't working, up until now . . . change was needed.

Two weeks before my birthday that year, August 30, I told the family I was living with, in short, succinct fashion, that I was going to sign up for long haul truck driving school and would be leaving them. They all took it pretty well, which left me a bit taken aback. Now I felt so small that my leaving wasn't up for debate. They did tell me several times how they didn't want me to leave, but I was very aware that I had really built things up in my thinking that just weren't there, and that I *had* to leave and take this next step, for my sanity.

Early on the morning of my departure, while still asleep in bed, my friend's older brother rushed into my room. "Wake up, wake up! Our neighbor needs CPR!" I jumped out of bed, threw on some clothes, and quickly followed my friend's brother to the neighbor's. We ran up the steps of the old trailer house to find the poor old man lying on the floor just inside the door, his face ashen and his hysterical wife begging him to speak to her. I immediately knelt next to him and started doing chest compressions. I kept telling him it was OK and kept his heart pumping until the paramedics arrived.

Sadly, the old man didn't make it.

As I look back on these life moments, it's surprising how comfortable I am with the process of life and death, but that's a story for another time. So, in "that" frame of mind, we returned to the house, and an hour later—bag in hand—I headed to the Greyhound bus station.

I always thought there was something so spiritual or other worldly, and also full circle about the fact that the way that I entered and left this particular time in my life was framed by death. With this in mind, while riding on the Greyhound bus, I was ready for my life's next chapter. This involved something I never thought. I, a gay man, would become—a long haul truck driver.

Looking back, I now have clarity. I made a decision on my own, for me, that changed my life. All it took was finally loving myself and not acting out of fear or self-preservation. I made a decision to act based on how I truly felt about what I was experiencing. Yes, once again I was leaving, but this time it wasn't out of fear, it was to preserve my self-respect. That changed *everything!*

I made it to the truck driving school in Lancaster, Texas, with more zest for life than I had felt in two years. Now, don't get me wrong—it wasn't a walk in the park. One day an angry classmate pinned our teacher against the wall and hit her before running out of class. That was interesting, to say the least! But I knew I was heading in the right direction.

I passed my test for the Class A driver's license on my second attempt and learned how to back up a 53-foot trailer without wrecking it or jackknifing. I had to drive a full month with a professional driver. Unfortunately, the driver they paired me with happened to be a homophobe who would scream at the top of his lungs that gay people are the devil. It also happened to be the same month gay marriage was legalized in the United States, and as a gay man, that added to the constant tension in the cab. I heard a bounty of slander over that month, but I just acted as heterosexual as I could to not get fired or worse, killed.

In the end, I persevered for my growth and happiness. I felt so happy and proud the day the company assigned me a truck of my own to drive. My first long-haul delivery was from Lancaster, Texas to Phoenix, Arizona. When I backed into that truck dock in Phoenix, I saw myself differently. I truly felt a sense of worth, accomplishment, and self-respect . . . earned *for* me *by* me.

For the next two years, nothing stopped me. I took every job I could, with the goal of seeing all of America. I saw everything I could from the seat of my truck. I drove through all forty-eight of the contiguous states and learned how to take care of myself in a way I never knew how to, before. From that time on, I have been true to myself and I learned how to enjoy my own company (in an eighteen-wheeler you really have no choice, haha). This was the happiest I'd been with my life since I was fifteen years old.

I left truck driving a few years later. It had taught me all it had to offer. My life continues its ups and downs. The experience of truck driving was one of the biggest turning points in my life! I've never been the same. My relationship with myself, my family and friends has improved dramatically. I'm stronger in every way: mentally, emotionally, and as a functioning member of society. Words of inspiration by Shannon L. Alder that I keep close . . . "One of the greatest regrets in life is being what others would want you to be, rather than being yourself."

TODD MILLER
Tucson, AZ

## *In the Nick of Time*

I HUNG UP THE PHONE on a warm day in March. The windows of my home were open, and there was a nice breeze with the sound of doves cooing outside. I had just received a pitch to purchase a real estate education program for several thousand dollars. The call had come out of the blue, and during the thirty minutes I spoke with the recruiter, I silently asked God and my angels for guidance. *Is this the right program for me?* The recruiter finally said to me, "Todd, if you don't do this now, you probably never will."

That was the straw that broke the camel's back. I made a quick decision to purchase the program, and with a modest down payment and monthly installments, I was on my way to something that I hoped would change my life. I thought, *no one has ever offered a payment plan,* noting that was the only way I could afford it. Little did I know this was just the beginning of the great success I had always held faith believing would come to me some day.

The recruiter explained to me how this six-week program was different from other programs because not only would it provide me with the fundamentals on how to become a real estate investor, but it would also provide a community of support, as well as teach me techniques on how to remove any internal blocks I might have concerning my relationship with money, how to use self-analysis to awaken my genius within, and how to live my life with a mindset of abundance versus one of poverty. Prayer and meditation were recommended throughout the coursework and beyond. That disclosure floored me. *Are you kidding me? A business course teaches all that?* I had never heard of such a thing. But it was right up my alley, and here's why:

Six months prior, in September 2020, in the midst of the pandemic, I was living on unemployment and stimulus checks after losing my sources of income. It was during this time when I had some sort of spiritual breakthrough. I started seeing sequences of numbers repeating over and over, for reasons I didn't understand. *What is this? Some sort of message from heaven?* I started feeling an awareness of not being alone, of being "watched over" and in a good way. In hindsight, I realize that a shift was occurring that would guide me to a higher dimension of living.

Sometimes things have to get ugly before they get better, and God had a plan for me to address some issues in my life before I could attain success in my entrepreneurial endeavors. I was finally taking my first steps toward a career in real estate. I had hired a mentor whose job was to guide me through my first deal—once I found one. He seemed a bit "gruff" on the exterior and had strict requirements, including for me to meditate and integrate other spiritual and grounding practices, like walks in nature and positive affirmations, into my daily life. That intrigued me, as I had been spiritually aware since I was a child, lost my spiritual awareness for a while and then regained it two decades ago. Though people saw me as this happy-go-lucky and inspirational guy, I was secretly dealing with a lot of hidden anger from both past and present events. I wondered how I could run a successful business with all this negative internal dialogue going on inside my head, which only added fuel to that fire called anger. I held hopes that my newly adopted meditation practices would help.

A month later, in October, I had a temper tantrum at a local mechanic shop over a two-hour job that had turned into a three-week nightmare. Halfway through the series of chaotic events being tossed my way, something shifted and I spontaneously went into a space of surrender. I asked myself, *What's really going on here? What is God or the universe trying to show me?* Then I realized the message was that I had to control my anger. I looked at my anger, made friends with it, and then it just melted away, and I fell into a place of peace and love. I literally started looking at everyone at the mechanic shop and the rest of the world through eyes of love.

After the three-week ordeal, I thanked the folks at the mechanic shop despite their shoddy workmanship and the damage they did to my car, for I felt true gratitude for the lessons I had learned. The shop manager apologized and said, "You inspire me." He saw my shift into a peaceful space with his own eyes. I continued to meditate and stay rooted in a space of gratitude and forgiveness. I kept listening to that little voice inside me that guided me to greener pastures. I had been praying for an emotional healing, and now my anger was pretty much gone. Of course, I do get annoyed at this or that from time to time, but I just send it through my heart chakra and neutralize it.

Fast forward to March 2021. I was still working with my mentor and had been driving through neighborhoods looking for boarded up and other distressed properties—which are half the homes in Tucson—knocking on doors, working my lead sheets, talking to people, looking for someone who would want to sell their beat-up home, so I could get it to one of my buyers, flip it, and make a profit. Six months in and no results. My unemployment would be running out in May, and I was determined to land a good deal before then. What was I missing? What was I doing wrong? I was soon to find out.

It was now time to begin my coursework and I was super excited. I decided to block out any negative thoughts and distractions and do exactly what I was instructed to do. I believed in this course, believed that its mentors held the key to the progress of my success. This was my chance, and I was committed to doing what they taught me, step by step.

Like I mentioned before, sometimes things have to get ugly before the beauty within can shine forth. I had no idea what was coming. I have always lived my life with tenacity, taking action and facing adversities head on, but what about the revelations that hide in the shadows, unknown, waiting to be discovered?

Starting with Lesson One, I learned the course was no joke. That is when I discovered my financial brokenness. It took me three weeks to complete that first lesson. Unfortunately, the course did not come with the disclaimer, *Make sure you have a therapist available on the sidelines.* Lesson One took me deep inside to face my relationship with myself, others, and the limiting beliefs I had about money. My beliefs were darker than I ever imagined. I was the oldest of five children, so you can say I sort of paved the way and remember more of our family's struggles than my younger siblings. My parents were young, and as you can imagine, no one taught them how to be financially smart, just as no one taught me. Robert Kiyosaki speaks of this in his books.

As children, we naturally view the world through a child's perspective, and when we see our parents fighting and struggling with money, as I did, we take on the belief that money equals pain, suffering, and strife, and through our subconscious minds, we push financial success away. I had several meltdowns during this lesson as I faced my financial demons. My younger sister, Sarah, had to act as my impromptu therapist, bless her heart. She has been my rock through the years. She would patiently listen without judging as I got everything off my chest. When it was all said and done, I can say that money and I are good now; I've cleaned up the negative subconscious views that surrounded my financial world.

As I continued with my coursework, one of the lead mentors of the group, Jamil, recommended I read the book "You are a Badass" by Jenn Sincero. I had listened to this author's first two books in my car. At first, my thoughts were, *Who is this chick with a raspy voice?* I almost dismissed the book as something that was not for me. But I continued to listen, thinking I could, maybe, recommend the book to someone else. After chapter two I was hooked! I went through her first two books, which significantly changed my life more than any books I have ever read. I was now not only learning more about living life with gratitude, but about this amazing practice called "manifesting," which is thinking and speaking your desired future into existence. I listened to the chapter on that subject over and over. I was determined to land a *big* deal before my unemployment ran out at the end of May.

Jenn's recommendation was to take massive action *now*, so I took her advice and immediately started looking for a life coach. Within thirty-six hours, the universe vibrationally lined me up with Laura Walker Coaching. Laura's energy and southern Texan accent were like comfort food to my heart and soul. I knew she would be the one to take me to the finish line of my immediate and future financial goals. I pulled out my credit cards, and we got to work.

I started the twelve-week Dream Builder course with Laura, and, as its name suggests, it was a dream come true. When Laura and I met I was unemployed, making some part-time deliveries, had hired a mentor, and to date had no deals in the oven. With her course, I learned about building my life by design and not living in default, about deserving my desires and bridging the gap between where I was and where I wanted to be. And yes, manifesting, too! I started feeding my faith more, starving and then befriending my fears. My dream—the dream I believed I deserved—was to start my own real estate business.

As I went through the course with Laura, I channeled my company name, "HS Property Solutions" (thank you, my angels), hired someone to help with my company logo and transform the design I drew up with pencil into the digital formats I needed. I hired the best photographer in town (thank you, Echo Star Maker), had business photos taken, and formed my LLC . . . all within four short weeks.

I have never been a thirty-year one-job person with a 401(k) that I hoped would sufficiently supplement my social security in retirement. Who wants to retire when you're living the life you love? I always knew in my heart that real estate would be my fortune, later in life. When, as the end of May drew near, my unemployment benefits were extended to mid-July, I saw it as proof that the universe works in its own due time and had my back.

One day late in May I received a phone call referring me to someone whose family member needed to sell their home right away. We arranged to meet, and during the meeting my phone rang with a desperate voice on the other line saying, "I'm going to be in foreclosure soon! Can you help me?" After eight long months of knocking on doors, sending letters, and talking to people, my phone finally started ringing. One thing led to another, and in eight short weeks I had multiple contracts signed. For how much, you ask? You guessed it, a total of $53,000 . . . three grand above my goal. In reality, I actually created $106,000 in income in those eight weeks, but I split it with my business partners and blew their minds. I visualized it and thus manifested it, and was now living by design, not by default.

I booked a plane reservation for the third week in July, one week after my unemployment was due to run out. I had opened my business account with the minimum deposit required. I had vowed to myself to have money in that account by the end of the month. I visualized myself closing at least one of my deals before I left to visit my family in Kentucky. I had a chat with God/the universe and let it be known that it was okay to have practically nothing in my account when I flew out of Tucson, but I chose to have money deposited by the time I woke up the day after arriving in Kentucky. Sure enough, my unemployment ended, we closed the deal late on Tuesday of the next week, and after making a stop at the night deposit box I flew out early Wednesday. When I woke up Thursday morning, I had manifested tens of thousands of dollars into my bank account. Just as I had asked . . . and just in the nick of time.

Special thanks to my mentors and support team: Laura Walker, Jenn Sincero, Jamil Damji, Gabriel Austin, Sarah Miller, Nathan Nesselroad, and everyone else who loved me during this amazing, trying and adventurous time in my life.

SHANNON PATTILLO
San Francisco, CA

# *Saying Yes to Me*

WHEN I WAS SEVENTEEN, I broke my neck in a car accident. It was a warm summer day before my senior year of high school, and it altered the course of my life. Looking back, I would not change a thing because that experience taught me so much.

You really realize the importance of true friendship when something like this happens. Throughout my long recovery process, I watched as people started to disappear from my life, one by one. All, but a handful of friends left me during that time. I learned how important it is to have truly good friends in your life, and how important it is to *be* a good friend.

As I navigated the long road to recovery, I discovered that I had an innate sense of strength that I didn't even know I had inside of me. A type of strength that isn't present in day-to-day life, but becomes fierce when faced with a life-altering experience or heartache.

I was very, very lucky to have survived this accident and make a full recovery, but it left me wondering what my purpose in life could be. I've spent much of my life pondering the answer to that question. I've gone through my life with considerable fear of failure, to the point where I'd quit something immediately, if I couldn't grasp it right away or if I wasn't good at it the first time.

As I aged, I realized that I had missed out on many opportunities because I was too afraid to try. I became extremely good at telling myself that I wasn't smart enough or capable enough to learn new things.

Even though I had a good job, I was still left feeling empty inside, and I had absolutely no idea of who I was and what I wanted. The irony was that I had no problem helping someone else or seeing the good in others, but I never hesitated to beat myself up. I had zero self-confidence. Self-worth? I seemed to be unable to know mine!

I finally got to the point where I was very uncomfortable in my own skin. Everyone around me was moving forward with their lives but I was left standing, watching them pass me by. I watched them move forward, embracing life and making changes, trying new things, sometimes succeeding, other times failing. Suddenly it became scarier for me to stay where I was in my life than it was to jump . . .

So, with a new boost of fresh perspective, I quit my job and moved back to the Bay Area, where I took time off to figure out what I wanted to do with my life. That is when I started researching life coaches. If I was going to start a new journey, I wanted to have a guide to support me with new tools and help me navigate the uncharted territory.

When I met Laura Walker for the first time, I knew she was the right one for me. We connected immediately through tears and laughter, as we got to know each other. However, it was not an easy road for either of us. The way I imagined it would work was that I would tell her my struggles and she would fix me. That *did not* go according to my plan. We almost fired each other at least twice! I was not easy to work with because, as I stated before, I was afraid of trying and didn't think I could do the work she was asking me to do. I remember throwing some choice words her way and having a couple of temper tantrums. Thankfully, she was patient and taught me how to change my thinking patterns.

This whole process was one of the most difficult, yet most rewarding, experiences I have ever been through. I learned over our time working together that it took a daily commitment to the tools she taught me, but it was worth the effort because it has changed my life.

Here are some of the positive changes that I have made in my life: I finally started to live for myself and put myself first. Through working with Laura, I have learned that I don't have to help everyone, don't have to please everyone, and that it's okay for me to say no. It's okay for me to try and it's okay if I fail. I have learned my worth and have started to see what the people in my life have always seen in me, but I was unable to see in myself.

I now have an amazing job working for and with the most wonderful people. With my bucket list in hand, I have slowly started checking things off. I am facing my insecurities and fears head-on and conquering them one day at a time.

In addition, a lifelong dream of mine has been realized. I volunteer weekly at the Marine Mammal Center in Sausalito, working alongside the most amazing group of people. I stepped way out of my comfort zone and am taking a pole dancing class! It is sooooooooooo hard, but it's okay, because it's for me and *my* growth.

I am now full of hope and a sense of adventure. Every day I am grateful, and the sky is the limit! A new chapter is opening, and I am so excited. I am so grateful for my life, for being able to be mom to my beautiful children, for my friends and family, and for all the opportunities that come my way.

I have finally realized that I deserve to be happy and live the life that I would love to live. I am using the tools I have learned to live a life that I love, and I will continue to enjoy the journey and learn all I can.

"*Up until now*" means something different for each story. For me, it's what I hear whenever an old thinking pattern comes to my mind. Saying it helps me stay focused on the life I have created by changing my thought process. I've learned how to say yes to *me*.

JAMIE SALERNO
Pensacola, FL

## *Grateful*

GRATEFUL IS HOW I FELT THAT DAY. Grateful that I had the awareness to listen and feel the calm that was washing over me, like a new sunrise displaying the beautiful pinks and purples of the day. I did not feel it immediately; it initially felt like Groundhog Day, and I was in a terrible movie that was playing over and over again. I felt completely deflated and scared at first. Little did I know what was around the corner.

I am an only child. I have an incredible connection with my parents, I can go to them with anything. My Mom dubbed us the "Three Musketeers." She always says, "We are small but mighty." My parents were high school sweethearts and have been married for forty-six years. They have always been my biggest fans and are supportive of everything I do, be it cheerleading, swimming, student council, tennis, or my work. It did not matter what it was, my parents were there. That sounds easy but logistically, it was not. We lived forty minutes east of my high school, Dad worked an hour and a half north and Mom worked an hour and fifteen minutes south. But no matter, they were always there.

Our house was always the fun house growing up. I had

awesome parties, sleepovers, and last minute get-togethers that were just downright fun. My parents were universally loved and so many of my friends also called them, "Mom" and "Dad." I was not spoiled; rather, my mom said I was "loved." I worked really hard on my grades and the reward would often be an item I desperately wanted. I earned the coolest tower radio that had dual cassettes, an equalizer, a turntable, and a glass door. I was so excited when we went shopping for that!

I take pains to recount our history so that you can understand just how instrumental my parents are to my being, my existence. My Mom had her first heart attack December 17, 2011. It was a Friday and Mom and I had gone Christmas shopping. We went to Chili's and splurged by having two of their house margaritas on the rocks, with salt. What an awesome day that was!! All was well, we finished shopping and she returned to her house and I to mine. I went to bed excited about the presents we had purchased and turned off my phone, per usual.

The next morning my boyfriend at the time, came into the bathroom with a panicked expression on his face and said, "You need to call your Dad right now." So, I did. That was only the second time I had ever heard my Daddy cry in thirty-five years. "Jamie, it's going to be ok, but I need you to come to the hospital, Mommy had a heart attack last night."

My world stopped. I shut down. *Wait, what?*

"Ok," I said, "I'm on my way over."

As we were driving, all the memories came rushing through my head like a movie. I was recalling moments with Mom that I had not thought about in years! I was seeing them so vividly and I was praying, "Not yet, God. I still need her." I was pleading in my mind for Him to please spare her.

We got there and I saw my Mom. Come to find out she had been there for hours; I had not received any of the calls as my phone was turned off. I saw her and of course I felt complete joy that she was still alive, but sadness as she did not look great. She was so tired and just flat out sick. I ran to her, tears running down my face, so happy that I could hug her, and she could hug me back. She had had a couple of stents put in that morning and they had saved her life. I stayed with her and did not leave her side all day.

I decided to go grab some food that evening and when I got back, I went into Mom's room in the Intensive Care Unit (ICU). As I walked closer to her bed she said, "Jamie, I need to tell you something and I need you to not freak out." *Oh, ok*, I thought, a feeling of trepidation starting to come, *What now?*

I looked around and realized that my Dad was not around, and my uncle was not there either . . . "What is it?" I said, starting to panic "Daddy is downstairs in the Emergency Room. He is having chest pains, so they wanted to check him out."

At this moment, I felt like I had just been wiped out by the largest, strongest wave. Like I was being sucked down, twisted and turned and I was flailing to get to the top but I just kept getting pushed back down. I was fighting for air, trying to get out from beneath the water. "Jamie," Mom called, I looked at her and snapped out of it. *I can breathe. I am ok. Focus, Jamie* I tell myself.

"Ok," I hear myself say, "I'll head downstairs."

If only it was that easy . . . There had been a shooting in the area and the hospital was placed on lockdown. I could not get into the ER to see my Dad. *Ok. Deep breath.* I tell myself. I am back to praying. "Please God, I cannot bear to lose both my parents today."

And that is when I felt it. I felt a sense of calm wash over me. I stopped and listened. It is not often that I feel an overwhelming sensation of peace, but I felt it that day and I held onto it. *It is going to be ok*, I thought.

Eventually, I was able to get in to see my Dad. I ran to him with tears rolling down my face and hugged him, it was déjà vu of that morning. The events of the morning and the thought of losing the love of his life had been too much. Thankfully, it was just a panic attack.

*Thank you, Jesus! Thank you, thank you!* I said over and over in my head. I left Dad to go back up to the ICU and explained to Mom what was going on, she visibly relaxed. Dad was released that evening and I stayed with Mom until she was released from the hospital two days later.

It was one of the hardest days of my life. I am immensely grateful to have *both* my parents make it through such a challenging ordeal. I am grateful to have felt the calm and peace and knew that it was God working through the Holy Spirit. I am grateful today as my parents are still with me; the "Three Musketeers" live to see another day!

JACKIE SCOTT
Bloomsburg, PA

## *Why Stop Now?*

FROM A YOUNG AGE I knew that I wanted to join the military. I didn't have a backup plan, I just knew that that was what I was going to do. Although I was diagnosed with what the doctor said was sports induced asthma; I played soccer all throughout middle school. It wasn't until my senior year in high school that I really started to train physically, for boot camp.

My anxiety towards running was so bad, I would get sick the night before. The anxiety was manifesting itself into a physical sickness that would literally stop me in my tracks.

I remember the day in Junior Reserve Officer Training Corps when I had my first reality check. I ran a couple hundred feet with my friends to the starting point of what would be a long run. When we arrived, I found myself hunched over behind the group, with two of my friends standing by for support. After the pause, I took it a little slower and continued running, starting my mile and a half course. I had stopped using my inhaler a few weeks back but I knew I was going to need it to finish this run in thirteen minutes or less, to be able to pass the physical fitness test for the service.

Every day I ran, going a little further each day, until eventually the sickness subsided. It became a habit. Before and after school I religiously completed a twenty-minute run around town. One particular day, I called my recruiter to check in and his three simple words were something I have always remembered and used as a tool to keep moving forward; "Why stop now?"

Why did I stop then? Months before that I couldn't even think about running without retching. Running a mile and a half in under ten minutes just wasn't on my radar then. I was just trying to make it, for the first few hundred feet. But I had achieved it. I worked through it one step at a time, one day at a time, then five minutes at a time. I now knew I would pass my physical fitness test.

But why did I stop? Why was I putting a limit on my success? If I had let my sports induced asthma define me or introduced myself to others as "Jackie with anxiety," I never would have gotten this far. I went on to run for over an hour that day. That hour-long run became a daily practice. It became something I looked forward to and actually enjoyed. At that point, I wasn't running for time, distance, or any goal I was trying to achieve. It was just for me.

Twelve years later, as I'm reflecting on the goals I have accomplished; I wonder what made it possible for me, then? Why was I able to "push" through the pain? Did I have more motivation or more determination when I was eighteen years old? Maybe it was more discipline or more willpower? With years of practicing personal development, it just didn't make sense to me. Shouldn't I have improved on those skills by now?

It wasn't the motivation. It wasn't determination, discipline, or willpower. While all of those were present and used to achieve my goal, none of those were what made my goal a success story. I had a vision. Something I wanted to achieve beyond myself. I didn't have a backup plan in case it didn't work out. I didn't have anyone telling me to take it easy or to consider other options because I couldn't do it with anxiety or asthma. I definitely was not listening to others or their doubt or taking on that doubt as my own. I did not have to work to "push through anything" or use my willpower to keep me working towards my goal. I wasn't pushing.

I was being pulled. I was being pulled by a vision greater than myself, greater than anyone's doubts projected upon me, greater than my fears and greater than my self-limiting beliefs.

Up until now, I thought dreams and goals took more work and willpower. That I just had to fight for or push towards them but I realized that any vision I had was easy to keep working towards if it was in alignment with who I am and who I want to become.

The day my recruiter asked me "Why stop now?" was DEFINING! It was the day I learned how to expand my limits to achieve greater things and allow more flow of abundance into my life, which I will be forever grateful for.

ABBIE HABERSKI
Odessa, FL

## *Feather From Heaven*

I OFTEN FIND MYSELF wishing I could go back in time. More specifically—wishing I could relive every moment with my dad. The memories of building snow forts together during our many long and chilly winters in Maine, play on a loop in my head daily. All the gardens he helped me to build and the plants within them that he taught me to take care of, as if they were babies. My first car, high school prom, graduation, every holiday, all the laughter, all the tears, every moment flips through my mind like they're stuck in a ViewFinder.

Then I'm back, sitting on the pavement of the hospital parking lot with my seventeen-year-old sister and my brother, only nine years old. Just holding onto each other, praying, while my mom was inside, all of us still unaware of what had happened.

Being my father's first daughter, I truly was "daddy's little girl." I can't even tell you how many times in my life people have said to me that I am the spitting image of him. He truly was my best friend and we shared a bond like no other. One of my biggest fears is losing my parents and on February 3, 2022, that fear became my reality. I had never thought I would lose my dad at such a young age and when he passed away, I was completely broken. I often thought to myself, *This can't be real. How could this be my life, everything was fine just a few days ago?* I felt lost, stuck, confused, empty, all of it, and more. Now that I have resumed "normal life" I continue to feel all of these things except it's more like carrying it around like a ball and chain attached to my ankle. If you have experienced grief, you know exactly what I'm talking about.

Although I feel all these emotions, I never once felt disconnected from him. Yes, I know he is no longer here in physical form, but I find him everywhere. I hear him say, "Hey kiddo," every day when I get home. I see him in the red cardinal that has taken a liking to our backyard. I find him in everything that is purple because that was his favorite color. In every dragonfly, yellow butterfly, every sunset, and everywhere that I go, he is there. He never left us and his guardian angel made sure we knew that, on the night that he passed.

As we are sitting in the hospital parking lot for what feels like three hours but is in fact, only thirty minutes, my little brother looks up into the sky and points. He says, "Abbie look, there's a white feather," and there it was. At 9:40 pm in the beam of the streetlamp was a single white feather slowly floating down, next to us. My heart sank. My brother had no idea what that meant but I had heard the belief that when a loved one is passing and their guardian angel is helping them to the other side, the angel would drop a white feather to earth. At this point, we still did not know that my father had passed but we knew there was a chance. I still maintained hope that he was okay, I prayed and begged him to stay, for God to keep him here.

Just moments later I spotted my mother exiting the hospital doors, a nurse on either side of her. I ran up to her and pled "He's okay, right?! Everything is, okay?" There was so much pain in her eyes, I didn't even recognize her. She just shook her head and said

"Honey..." I knew she couldn't find the words. I was immediately overwhelmed by an all-encompassing terrible feeling. Numbness quickly took over my body, followed by unexplainable sadness and anger. I became angry with God and the Universe. *How could you take a father away from his children, a husband away from his wife? What did I do to deserve this?* I had all these thoughts and even though I had already gotten my first sign from him, I couldn't look past the pain I was feeling to see any of it.

As the weeks drifted by, he sent more signs. He was communicating with me in so many ways and I was opening myself up more and more to receive his messages. Songs would play in moments that made me think he was speaking to me through them. A red cardinal or dragonfly would suddenly appear anytime I was thinking about him. I started having extremely vivid dreams where he and I would have real conversations about things that were going on in my life at the time. He then started leaving me little "gifts" to find. The first was a "Tree of Life" pendant for a necklace that I found late at night. The Tree of Life was a symbol that my father loved. He had actually bought my mom a Tree of Life necklace years ago. I believe he wanted me to have one too. Another time I went to Costco and as silly as it may seem, I left in uncontrollable tears reminiscing on when my parents first went there and all the pictures my mom took of my dad holding up the oversized items that he thought were so cool. It was so simple but he found so much joy in it. As I was walking out, still crying, my partner picked up something off the ground and handed it to me. It was a rock, painted purple and yellow with the word "Smile" on it.

I continue to get signs from my dad every day. Through all his messages, big and small, I realized that he is still guiding me through life as much as he can. I realize how grateful I am to have the twenty years I was able to spend with him and to have all the amazing memories I have. He taught me so much in his time here and I will carry those teachings with me throughout the rest of my life. Will I always wish we had more time? Of course! But I feel beyond blessed to call him my father, he really was the best dad in the entire world and continues to be, on the other side. February 3 may have been the day that my dad left this earth, but he never left me.

CYNTHIA A MCQUADE-BRINKMAN
Brooklyn Park, MN

## *Morning Prayers*

MY MORNING PRAYER was often, "God, I don't want to be alive, find a way to kill me today." As early as my pre-teen years I dreamt of ways to commit suicide. From pills to self-harm, to guns, to being crushed by a car. I was often too afraid to try, and when I did, I was wildly unsuccessful.

In my twenties, I came to the realization that I probably would never be successful at suicide. That is when my prayers for God to remove me Himself began. I felt like a burden, an emotional basket case that caused more harm than good. The proof was all around me from childhood.

I kicked my brother in the balls, chased him with a chainsaw and an ax. I smashed a girl's head into the trunk of a car. When I wanted to be mean, I formed words that cut like a diamond on glass. When I hated me, I hated you. Once I calmed down, the guilt, shame and embarrassment consumed me. I would beg for forgiveness, and then vow, if God kept me alive until morning, to never be rageful again.

But the rage never left. From fits of yelling, to throwing a frying pan at my husband's head, to insane road rage while racing around the city with my son in the car. Perhaps laughable if you're watching dark comedy, truly traumatizing if you are on the receiving end. The shame of rage ate at me from the inside out. Rage is unacceptable outside of movies, it is unforgivable. I loathed the person I was and knew the work I was doing to heal couldn't cleanse the hatred within, or the judgment of the observer from without.

Looking at my life objectively, I see I didn't have it easy, but others had it worse and didn't behave like me. Forgiveness wasn't a luxury I would ever allow myself to experience.

As a young child I was sexually assaulted by multiple people, in multiple ways. My house burned down when I was six, my dad was an alcoholic. I learned from an early age the power behind sex secrets. In college, I was raped. In my first marriage, a pastor told me that I had to submit to my husband and allow him to have sex with me whenever he chose.

I was roofie raped in my thirties and by the time I was approaching fifty, I realized I had been sexually assaulted every decade of my life. Bottling rage was a habit. One of my perpetrators told me to lie about what had happened or someone would surely die. From the sizzling of the clover on the electric fence, to stories of how it would look like an accident, I believed I had to lie.

I hate lies. But I always lied to myself about my pain.

As I aged, I knew telling my story wouldn't kill people, intellectually I knew, but not viscerally. Every time I found myself being a victim of sexual assault, or other abusive behavior, I felt I had to remain silent and figure it out. I blamed myself. Those words of my voice having the power to kill someone were ingrained in my mind. The words were powerful lies. So powerful in fact, a phrase I often used was, "it's not like anyone is going to die" when referring to a simple task I was avoiding. I didn't know I was doing my best to stay alive. I only knew the shame of my actions made me want to die.

Changing that story in my body, mind and spirit has been a work in progress. For thirty years I have chased after healing the rage within. I've done a lot of work, but a major game changer was waking up and saying, "Grateful. Grateful. Grateful" despite the fact that I was wanting to say, "if it be your will God, could I slide off the bridge today?"

Grateful.

Grateful.

Grateful.

The more I practice, the more joyful my life is. The easier it is to forgive that battered child for being cruel to her brother. The more I can allow myself to forgive the abusive adult I had become as a result of unhealed childhood trauma.

The word gratitude, even if I couldn't feel grateful for being alive—gave me life. The words of encouragement from mentors, friends, and especially my beloved husband who was the recipient of a flying frying pan, gave me hope.

For over twenty years, I have had a Dream of building a resort. I have seen this resort as a place of healing, laughter, love and learning. It's the safe place I would escape to in my own mind, when I hopped on a horse and ran wild in the open field, away from the places I was abused and freely breathing fresh air. The resort is the place my imagination would venture off to, while drawing or staring at the creek bed while laying on the trunk of the tree crossing its path, dreaming of someone rescuing me from the painful moments of life. I dreamed I could build a resort that was a real healing place.

Yet, because of shame, I didn't think I was a worthy recipient to have that dream as my own. I gave that dream away as often as I prayed for God to take me away from this world.

*Up Until Now!*

Now, I have several "someones" who believe in me. I have

learned to hold fast to the dream through incredible coaches and mentors. I know I am supported. I know I am worthy to live a life in which I forgive myself. I allowed the journey toward my resort to take root in the spring of 2021. That is when I started a non-profit organization that is on a mission to provide hope for the hurting. It took faith, but faith didn't come before hope.

Faith is the substance of things hoped for, the evidence of things unseen. Substance is what we work with every day, and when we are guided by hope to point us to substance, we can receive healing in every area of our lives. I am living the life of my dreams and pointing others toward hope and assisting them in living out their dreams.

Now, I wake up grateful. I wake up knowing I have a purpose and I know my story does not define me, but it is worth sharing, so others who are hurting can find hope, build faith and lean into the substance that brings dreams to fruition.

PATRICK BLAHA
Fort Worth, TX

## *Finding My Place In Life*

GRADUATION WAS NEARING, and I was preparing to leave what some call, "the best years of your life" firmly behind me. My time at Stephen F Austin State University had definitely lived up to the adage, but it was time to put more focus on my future and start planning for the next phase of life. I had acquired a BBA in Accounting, and my plan was to move to Colorado. I did have a job offer there, but the pay was barely more than I made at a retail clothing store I worked at, during college. So, I opted to return to my hometown (in Texas) and accepted employment with a local CPA firm. Unbeknownst to me, my parents were preparing to move overseas, and as life would have it, they wanted me to live in their home, so that it would not be empty. This would be a win-win situation for me and my parents.

As I settled into my new beginning with the CPA firm, I quickly realized that this would not be a long-term gig. The feeling I got was that they were using me to get through tax season. As suspected, tax season came to an end, and I wound up without a job. I was feeling a tad disheartened, but another opportunity was around the corner.

I began work with a Marine Company that did maintenance work and engine overhauls on shipping vessels. It was an interesting job, and I did enjoy it and the people I worked with. What had started as a local "mom and pop" business, had become part of a global organization based in Sweden. This was exciting to me, because it offered more growth and advancement opportunities. This opportunity, however, was not without issue, as I was soon to find out. The prior owners remained a staple in the business, and tried to run the division as if it were still their own. My responsibilities were payroll and accounts payable. One day I came in to work, and the office was being remodeled. I found this odd, considering a little remodeling work had just been completed at the office six months prior. Nonetheless, I did my job, and did it well. Maybe a little too well! While processing payables, I noticed a bill to a remodeling company. Not unexpected, considering the office was being remodeled, but it raised a red flag because I knew that that particular company had not done work at the office. The work that was done by them was at the prior owner's home. I questioned this in a casual way and could tell by the response I received that the prior owner's wife knew I was on to them. I saw the writing on the wall. And a short time later, as predicted, I was once again, unemployed.

*What now?* I had considered Real Estate, but the thought of a total 100% commission career, in an industry I knew nothing about, terrified my young mind. While at the Marine Company, we utilized a payroll processing firm. I contacted them to see if they needed help since I was already familiar with their systems. They did not, but a couple of their management had left and started another payroll processing company. The new company was adding clients, and so, the next phase of my career began.

From day one, things were not adding up. Have you read the book "The Firm?" I found myself in a similar, less than desirable, situation. One day I overheard a conversation about arms deals. At that point, I knew I had no option but to get out. The day I got a call from an FBI investigator solidified this fact.

Willing to do anything, or go anywhere to get away from this company, I wound up in Waco, going to work for a bank. Just my luck, that nagging feeling that something wasn't right soon pushed its way to the forefront. Certain upper management was involved in questionable practices. *How was I the unlucky one to uncover this? What was I to do?* You know where this is going, as things unfolded, I was the scapegoat and found myself once again without a job.

However, it wasn't too long before I landed a position in the credit department of a pharmaceutical distribution company. Things were looking up! Real estate was still in the back of my mind, but the pharmaceutical company offered guaranteed income with growth plans laid out. I had a great boss. We were going to get this division in order, he was going to be promoted to a regional position and I would be promoted into his current position as Credit Manager for the division. I was happy to finally be in a good place. Until I wasn't. While going through files, my boss and I discovered that the regional position he had been promised was in the process of being eliminated. And the Division President knew this when he offered my boss the Credit Manager position, that was ultimately supposed to be my position. This was just the tip of the iceberg of discoveries of how this particular division was being run.

*How could this be happening AGAIN? What kind of black cloud was following me around?* My spirits were down, I was depressed, and knew something had to change. I decided accounting/financial positions were not what I wanted, and what I did want was to be in sales. Just not real estate. *Why was real estate popping into my mind again? It was too risky being 100% commission-based, with no benefits.*

I embarked on a career in medical sales, primarily mail order companies, specializing in the home delivery of medical disposables. Things were great, and over the next ten years my career grew with a couple of different companies. I was promoted to management to oversee a sales team in the Midwest and moved to Ohio. A corporate merger brought me back to North Texas, and the "black cloud" began to slowly rear its ugly head. Thanks to corporate politics I found myself sans a job, again! To amplify my anxiousness, my savings were dwindling, as time passed. It was taking a toll on me mentally. *What was I going to do? How was I going to survive?* I felt my life was going nowhere, and I had nothing to show for all my years of working.

That inner voice kept pushing me towards real estate. Only this time, the feeling was much stronger. I started real estate classes while continuing to interview for medical positions. I was comfortable in the medical field, and it did provide a guaranteed income and health benefits. One day, I received a call from a recruiter. I was told that I had been selected for a management position with a company based in Florida. I was so excited. The long search had ended, and I would be back in management. All we had to do was finalize the process and select a start date. A week later, I was told things had changed and "the company was going in a different direction." I was devastated. I resolved that that was the last search I would make for a position in the medical industry. I had to take charge of my own life.

I finally listened to my inner voice, obtained my real estate license, and have never looked back. I say this was God "slapping me in the face" to listen to Him and follow His direction. My career in real estate has thrived, I obtained my broker license, and I'm with an organization that has so much to offer. I train new agents and am putting things in place to build my team. Perhaps one day, I will have my own brokerage. My success in real estate has allowed me to get out of debt, build up savings and travel the world. I couldn't be happier, and I only wish I had listened to my inner voice long ago.

The point of my story is, no matter what you are going through, do not give up. Keep fighting. We all have our own journey. We cannot compare ourselves to others, as our paths in life are different. I definitely had my employment struggles, and the emotional and mental aspect of that did take a toll. But each experience helped shape who I am today. Keep the faith, and listen to that inner voice or gut feeling. It may well be God's way of directing you to better things in life. We just have to be open to His message and keep the faith. They say when you enjoy your work so much that it doesn't feel like work, you are in the right place. That is how I feel about my career in real estate. Unbeknownst to me, my past experiences were preparing me (in ways I only now realize) for the amazing career I have in this field. Case in point: the analytical aspect from accounting for preparing a market analysis and reviewing contracts. Also, my past management experience has come in handy, now that I am managing my own team.

I always wanted to have my own business. And now I do. Just not in the manner in which I thought I wanted. Instead, in the way I am supposed to have it. So, remember your dreams and don't be afraid to go after them. Forget the naysayers. All you have to do is believe in yourself and fight for your dream. You have that dream for a reason. Most importantly, keep the faith. Listen to God's message, and He will direct you. And always be grateful for what he has provided. Now, go after your dream!

SHARON BRYANT
Arlington, TX

## *Time For Change*

THE OTHER STUDENTS made fun of the fact that my parents were older. They liked to tease me about my glasses being so thick. I'll never forget it and the way it made me feel. I hated my life and was so sad. I loved my parents and my family, but I did not have anyone I could talk to about the sadness that was consuming me deep inside. I kept everything bottled up inside. My self-esteem bottomed out.

I grew up the youngest of eight children and by all accounts, we were a very poor family. I wanted to please everyone, even to my own detriment. As for myself, I didn't think I deserved any happiness. I'm not sure why, but I remember that's how I felt and my inner dialogue reflected that exact level of unworthiness. I did okay academically but struggled socially. As life went on, I became a high school math teacher and was successful in the classroom for thirty plus years. I loved teaching but deep down I felt that something was missing. I retired from teaching, sincerely thinking that this was all life had in store for me.

After enjoying retirement for a bit, I began to explore options and explore ideas that were being whispered to me deep down. In

2017, after looking into what I could do, to generate some income and have fun in retirement, I became a realtor and started to see some success. But still that nagging feeling that something was missing persisted. I love helping others but I was noticing a pattern where I rarely received help for myself. The funny thing is, I did not know that I needed help, I wasn't "awake" enough to have that awareness! The last couple of years have been tough on everyone, my family and my emotional and mental health were no exceptions to the struggles. We were faced with a worldwide pandemic [COVID-19] and what seemed like the end of the world as we know it. *Up until now. . . .*

I went with a friend at her invitation to a Women's Empowerment Luncheon. It was a wonderful opportunity to mingle with other realtors, lenders, and other professionals. The speaker that day was Laura Walker, a transformational life coach. As she spoke about longings and discontents, she asked the ladies what they would love their life to look like. I began to realize I was missing something and she had the tools I had been longing for deep down. This may sound bold, but she was the answer to my prayers. I started working with Laura and as we put tools in my toolbox and I learned how and when to use these tools, life began to change drastically. Slowly I started to understand that I needed to please myself and dream big, asking myself what would I LOVE my life to look like? I now know that I deserve success in all the areas of my life.

As I transformed on the inside, my life personally and professionally began to transform organically on the outside! I began selling more homes and it seemed effortless, as though someone had given me the "easy button." Success started following me without my pushing, grinding and working hard for it. I started giving more of my talents and resources. Whenever an opportunity arose to give food, money, kindness, I GAVE. Thank You, God for sending me to that luncheon. My thinking changed and my life changed with it, for the better! God has so much in store for us! Most people never tap into that divine Truth. I started thinking and believing more in myself. My life started changing. Everyone started noticing my transformation and mentioned it to me, it felt amazing. Day by day and step by step my life transformed for good!

JUDY COOPER
Lake Oswego, OR

## *Courage*

LIVING WITH MY GRAN at six years old was an adventure, but little did I know that that "adventure" would have us come face to face with a dangerous man.

The day started out pleasant enough. Sunny and carefree, I had enjoyed playing with my group of friends in the wide, tree lined streets of a small town in New Jersey. Eventually the day wore down and my friends wandered back to their respective homes, bringing an end to the fun.

As I entered Gran's house, I happily made my way through the kitchen and into the hallway catching a glimpse of events that were unfolding.

Gran was on the bed laying on her back, her legs dangling off the edge of the bed. Her boyfriend, Les, was bent over her with his back towards me, his hands around her neck choking her. I heard Gran desperately begging him to stop! Oblivious to any consequences, I thrust myself into the situation by shouting, "Don't you hurt my grandmother!" while hitting him in the back. Before I could comprehend what was happening, I soared through the air, placed next to gran on the bed, with his hands around my throat. I found myself face to face with him, with nowhere else to look but into his bulging eyes and the swollen red veins in his neck. That vision is forever etched into my memory! Gran successfully coaxed my release from his grip and told me to go to bed.

I wandered back to my bedroom with some dread, unable to let go of the fear I still harbored for her. I ran to the downstairs kitchen, pulled over a chair and climbed over the sink area, and out the basement window. My intention was to connect with a neighbor for help. I stumbled across to the neighbor's yard where he was chatting with a friend. Quickly, I engaged his help. Although alarmed to see and hear what I described, he briefly discussed with his friend on "how best to proceed." It was decided between them that he would walk around the house listening for activity, peer into any window to assess the level of danger. His friend would stay with me.

The neighbor walked back and explained to us he had determined enough time had passed that he thought it was safe to return. He took my hand in his, I began to feel a sense of relief that this incident could be over. He walked me home and knocked on the front door. We both stood there anxiously waiting for the door to open only to be greeted with a surprised look from Les. After all, he expected me to be in bed. I suddenly realized that I might be in a LOT of trouble! The neighbor briefly explained my concern to Les, who waved me back into the house. In the end, no one ever spoke of that incident again. In fact, I never saw Les again!

Once the event was over, the emotional aftermath descended, taking over my thoughts. The events that unfolded that day destroyed my sense of security. The active threat to my Gran and myself, left me struggling with many upsetting emotions. At the age of six I didn't understand this "adult world." I was overwhelmed with guilt, feelings that my world was no longer safe, and feelings of total helplessness in it! I often struggled with these emotions. I became withdrawn, anxious with fear taking over. Suffering in silence, lost in my head, these intrusive feelings stayed with me throughout my growing up years, well into adulthood.

I knew I needed help to resolve these emotional issues/traumas, but when one is feeling "alone" you don't know how or who to reach out to, for help. At this point my need for resolution was greater than holding onto my issues, so I opened up to a friend. That decision proved to be a momentous one as well as a pivotal point in my mental health journey. It was during this conversation that I discovered that there was another dimension to my "story." As I poured my heart out, she listened intently, wide eyed, gasping at the physical attack, then she expressed deep empathy for me. She then shared that it was a horrific story, she was glad that we had survived but she went further to say, how inspiring it was even though it was horrible. My display of "fearlessness" at six years old against an adult man, several times larger than myself was amazing to her! How courageous it was for me to take such initiative to protect my Gran. I was perplexed by her reaction, which gave me pause.

Being vulnerable about a painful chapter in one's past, staying open to receiving her words of enlightenment became a huge pivotal moment!

Realizing that there was another way to view the "story" beginning as a tragic story but with an inspirational ending was quite a different story to tell my inner critic, but also in the telling of this tale to others. The realization that I could alter my perception of myself with this alternative viewpoint really did change my inner dialogue about myself. Previously I never viewed myself as courageous but the new me had a boost of confidence and pride. That meant the old storyline was no longer gripping me or holding me back!

KIRSTEN FAGAN
Semmes, AL

# *I Choose Joy*

"IF I EVER CATCH YOU on the street, I will kill you!" Those words sent a chill down my spine. No one had ever said anything like that to me before and quite honestly, I never wanted to hear those words ever again.

I was reaching a point where I was longing for a new career, a place where I felt secure, valued, and successful. A place where my love for others could shine and I would not be teased for being "too kind" or "too loving." I felt utterly defeated. I truly felt as if there was no way something like that was available to me.

Until one day a small quiet voice said, "You can do whatever you set your mind to! If you want *more*, then go get it."

You see, as a little girl my parents always told me, "You can do whatever you set your mind to." I always thought they were just being loving, supportive parents but it wasn't until I got older that it really sunk in and I realized how much truth my Dad and Mom had spoken into me. I could be and do more!

Life felt heavy as an adult. My husband and I worked very hard, but money always seemed to be incredibly tight. We both pooled our resources and got our Bachelor's degrees but we still had aways to go and I, like many others, was struggling to figure out what to do with my degree.

I had worked hard and moved into a better position, but still felt like there was more out there for me. One day my employer came to me and said, "Kirsten the state regulations have changed . . ." My head began to spin. I knew exactly what that meant. I would soon be out of a job.

I had been thinking about trying to find a way to work from home but was questioning myself, *was I really ready? Could I create the income my little family required to live?* The thoughts raced through my head and I just wasn't sure. All the insecurities and ugly words I had heard from others came creeping in. I was scared. *I am a mom, wife, and dog mom. How can I possibly support myself and my family with my own business? We depend on this income*, I thought. The thought of attempting something new after fourteen years at the same job was terrifying, to say the least.

As I drew close to the end of my employment, I took the leap and opened my own business. It was the craziest, scariest, and most exciting thing I had ever done in my life! Money was tight and I did not know how we were going to make it, but somehow, we did.

I taught myself how to coupon, garden and can food. When I wasn't working hard to feed my Family, I was working hard on trying to figure out how to make my business a success. I spent hours googling free apps, programs and other business-related needs. And slowly I started gaining clients. But things were still far from ideal.

After two years of having my business, I still wasn't quite making what I would have loved to make financially (to be honest, I was pretty far from it). I began to wonder if I would need to do something else, but I knew that working from home and being available to my two little girls was exactly what I wanted to do. And that small voice inside me kept whispering, *keep going!* I still felt fear—fear of the unknown and of failure, but I decided to continue putting energy into building my vision of a successful business.

Suddenly, all the pieces started to fall into place. One day, I reconnected with a beautiful friend from high school and I quickly realized how much I had needed her friendship. It felt like no time had passed and she always knew just what to say, to make me feel empowered. We ended up working together for many months and then one day she called me and we had a conversation that forever changed my life. In that conversation she introduced me to a life coach she knew.

In no time at all, I began working with my first life coach. She was (and is) beautiful inside and out and it just felt good to work with her. She radiated positivity and joy and those were two things I really wanted in my life. As we worked together, my life began transforming rapidly and I began getting clarity on what I wanted to do with my business and how I wanted to help others. I began seeing coaches on social media and thought, *I would love to work with her*, or *Wow, wouldn't it be awesome to work with some of these other coaches . . .*

About a week after seeing one coach's profile and realizing I wanted to meet her, I was introduced and immediately began working with that very coach. I was floored! *How did this happen?* And was it a fluke? Suddenly, coaches started reaching out to me, I could hardly believe what was happening.

One day as I was talking to a coach she said, "Kirsten, you manifested this! You got your mind where it needed to be and with help from your higher power you were able to manifest exactly what you wanted and you're not done."

Her statement and the conversations that followed blew me away and I realized she was right. I started thinking about my parents and the words they had always spoken to me about doing whatever I put my mind to. I quickly realized the deeper meaning to their words and began to feel so much gratitude. They were right, I can do whatever I want! And you know what? I am not done yet!

LAUREN GIULIANI
Boerne, TX

# *From Fired to Teacher of the Year (Almost)*

I HAD NOT EVEN turned my classroom lights on, that Monday morning when my email pinged and my heart dropped into my stomach. "Concerns" burnt along the subject line, my fingers shook as I had to open it—my principal only sent emails with that title when I had done something that, in his mind, was "egregious."

My mind immediately started running through everything I could think of that had happened in the past week that could possibly be construed as "wrong." *Did I say something to that one kid that hurt his feelings?* or *Did I put a grade in for that one girl that her parents were not okay with?*

I held my breath as I read the email that asked me to meet with him and my vice-principal after school that day, with no clarification as to what the concerns were. They wanted me to wait the ENTIRE day and continue to act like nothing was wrong—there was no way that was going to happen. I dropped my bags and tore down the hallway. "Have you seen Mr. Smithman?" I questioned people as my voice cracked. My knees were trembling as I walked up to him and began to ask what the concerns were, his response was just, "we will talk after school, now is not the time." My fear turned to anger, and tears begun streaming down my face. His eyes got wide, he said, "Why don't you take the day, and come back this afternoon." I couldn't even speak, I just nodded and walked back to my classroom, defeated, attempting to conceal my emotions.

I didn't care at that point; the bell had rung, and students were piling outside my door waiting for the first period. I could hear them chattering about their weekend, until they saw my face. Their reaction was not to ask what was wrong, but to run over and hug me. I loved that about my middle school students, they trusted me and knew I cared. I told them I was fine. I quietly packed my things and walked out of my room, I cried as I walked to my car. I called my mom and she told me to go home, she would drive down from her home for the day. I was blessed that my parents only lived about forty-five minutes away from me, at that point.

That day was a blur, all I could do was replay every action of the past week in my head. When 3:45pm came around, I held my breath again as I walked into my vice-principal's office where she and Mr. Smithman were seated, waiting for me. My stomach was in knots, this was only my second year as a teacher and the school had been a rough place to jump into as a young teacher. The conversation of that meeting brought up accusations that were so outlandish to me. In summary, they believed a teacher who had shared negative information involving me, and when I inquired as to the teacher's identity, they would not tell me. My mind was racing, I heard Mr. Smithman say, "teaching is a lot about finding the right fit," he paused, "and we just don't think you are the right fit for this school." I picked my head up and said, "That's fine, I do not want to be here anyway." We discussed that I would finish out the year and then find a new school for the next year.

I was at peace, until that Thursday, April 15, 2021, when I received an email from human resources at the Central Office. Subject line: "Employment Concerns." *What now?* I thought to myself.

They wanted to meet the next morning, but that was not going to fly. I got in my car and sped over to the Central Office.

I opened the door and demanded to speak to the Assistant Superintendent. He walked down and we met in a large, ugly, yellow room. He told me to not worry, he tried to keep me calm, but the more he spoke, the more heated I got. He told me to report to the Central Office the next Monday morning, and to not go back to the Middle School that I taught at. By the end of the next week, I was told by the Central Office that I needed to find a new school district to teach at for the next year—all because of things that never even happened!

I was an emotional wreck, my poor family and boyfriend had no idea what to do with me. As I sat with my mom, in the pool, tears ran down my face, I felt like such a failure. "How can I help make you, okay?" my mom questioned, I shrugged, since I didn't think anyone, or anything could help. "I am going to give your information to a friend of mine named Laura, she is a life coach and I think she could help you." The pair of them had been sorority sisters in college and had recently reconnected. In retrospect, I now see that this was a "God thing" because their reconnection was God working to get me in a better place, in my life.

I had my discovery session with Laura later that week, within that first hour meeting with her, I felt more at peace for my future. Laura's voice and demeanor was something that I needed in my life at that point. By the end of that session, I had committed to starting my Dream Builder journey with her. "What is the life you would love?" She would ask me. Automatically my mind said, "I want a teaching job that I love, and I want to be teacher of the year." That was the life that I would love to live. With Laura's help, I out my vision statement. I envisioned myself being a great teacher, despite what I had gone through, just a few months before.

"I choose to radiate love, joy and gratitude. I am free to create a life I love living, and make welcome all things that are for my highest and greatest good. Every day, I embrace my true power and take control of my life. I do not see failure, only feedback and stepping stones for my Future."

I would begin my day with affirmations and reading my vision statement every day, and in May I walked into a new school for my interview. My knees shook as I waited outside the principal's office, but I kept saying my affirmations over and over. I walked in and instantly felt at ease. I anxiously awaited the call, and I expected to wait a few days, at least. However, that evening my phone rang! "We would like to offer you the position," I heard my new principal, Mr. Lewin say. I was so giddy as I accepted it.

I knew this was going to be a new fresh start, but I still had fears (thanks to my previous school situation) as I prepared for the new school year. *What would I love?* I continued to ask myself, I knew that I wanted to be an amazing teacher. I had spent so much time thinking that I was a failure because of everything that had transpired at my last school, but I was reminded that "my past does not have to be my future" and I had to constantly remind myself that I was not a failure, but rather all of this was a stepping stone to even better things.

Even before I started the year, I had been asked to join a committee! The situation was a complete 180 from where I had been four months prior. It was finally time to begin the year, and I was a mix of nerves and excitement, simultaneously! I walked into the school and Immediately, was at ease, I decorated my classroom to perfection as I anxiously awaited the arrival of my new students.

"I am Teacher of the Year," I said every single morning on my way to work, and I lived it at work. My mindset was completely different than it had ever been. I was excited to go to work, whereas, before I met Laura, I actively dreaded going to work. By the middle of the year, I was Student Council advisor, Junior FFA advisor, on the Instructional Focus Team, and was nominated by my peers to the District Wide Advisory Committee. I was on fire, and I could feel the difference in everything. It was almost as if my mind had reprogrammed, and I was able to "change the channel" in my head, if there was something that did not align with my vision.

"You're my favorite teacher!" "I love your class, Miss!" "You make learning fun!" My students reassured me that I was doing a good job, and it felt so good. I felt myself growing as a teacher.

"I am Teacher of the Year" I said constantly, that was my vision. I attributed my attitude towards my vision to my time in Dream-Builder, and I knew that I needed to grow even more. I decided to invest in myself even more and started "Working with the Law" to understand the Laws of the Universe, because *up until now* I had thought I understood how the universe worked. But with a deep dive into each Law, I could see and understand the world so much clearer. I started using the Laws and found a partner-in-believing at work. She helped remind me anytime I got into a negative mind space, "where energy flows, energy goes," to change my channel of thinking.

March rolled around and it had been such a different experience than, what I was accustomed to. I loved my job, even on the hard days!

"TEACHER OF THE YEAR NOMINATIONS" plastered the subject line of a new email. My heart dropped and I got so excited, my vision kept popping up in my head. "I am teacher of the year." I began using my vision statement religiously and knew that I had earned it.

"What do you do to help the community?" my partner in believing asked me. I was confused as I told her, and she replied, "well I have to know so I can fill in the nomination!" My heart skipped a beat, it was actually a possibility. Then a second teacher came and asked the same thing, then a third. "Seriously?!" I thought to myself as it started to sink in that it was a possibility. I was so honored to just be nominated, it was my first year in the district and people already saw the potential in me, to become Teacher of the Year.

Two weeks later, the results arrived in my inbox . . . and I had one of those flash moments of nervousness and excitement. I clicked the email, and . . . I had *not* gotten the Teacher of the Year position.

Up until working on my vision and understanding the "Law of Thinking," I probably would have been completely upset, but I now was able to re-shape my thinking. I had come from being asked to leave my last school, to being nominated for Teacher of Year at my new school. It was an unthinkable change, and ultimately, I was happy I didn't win, it gave me time to get even better so I could come back and take the title the next year.

That same week that I learned the results, I was at a meeting and Mr. Lewin and he told me, "We need a new Department Head for math next year, and we would like you to take that position, are you interested?" He had barely finished his sentence when I blurted out, "Yes." I now had a leadership position for the 2022–2023 school year.

*Up until now*, I thought that I had no control over my future, but now I am ready for anything the universe throws at me!

RENEE HILL, PH.D.
Fort Lauderdale, FL

## *From Poverty to Ph.D.*

ALL MY LIFE, I was a "good girl." I loved school—even skipping a grade and graduating from high school at sixteen; I went to church every Wednesday and twice on Sundays (and actually enjoyed it!); I was an only child who was responsible, trustworthy, obedient, and didn't give my parents trouble. So, imagine my abject terror to find myself pregnant during my sophomore year of college at the tender age of seventeen. To say that I was ashamed of myself was putting it mildly. After all, what kind of God-fearing Christian *has a child out of wedlock*? To make matters worse, from the time he learned I was pregnant, my child's father alternated between telling people that I was a liar, denying our relationship, and trying to coerce me into terminating the pregnancy.

My shame about my situation led me to hide my condition from my parents, and because I did, I was unable to ask for their support in order to get prenatal care and more nutritious food than the cheeseburgers, pizzas, and sodas I consumed on a daily basis. Desperate to ensure the health of my baby, I searched for help. This was 1992, well before Google and high-speed internet made it possible to have answers within seconds of starting a search, so my information seeking came in the form of asking friends and acquaintances what I should do.

Eventually, I was pointed in the direction of what at the time was called "HRS: Florida's Department of Health and Rehabilitative Services." There, I applied for and received food stamps, Medicaid, and cash assistance. I was officially "on welfare." Even though I knew I needed the help that public assistance provided, accepting this type of aid brought on a fresh round of shame. As far as I knew, no one else in my family had relied on the government for help—not even my maternal grandparents who had been dirt poor and still managed to raise nine children without joining the welfare rolls.

Thankfully, my pregnancy progressed perfectly and eventually, of course, I told my parents about my condition. Though they were initially shocked and upset, they were also concerned and supportive, even taking care of my son so that I could return to school and be a "normal" college student. I was grateful for this amazing help from them, but I quickly realized that I needed to be with *him*, so I transferred to a university closer to my hometown and moved back in with my parents. I continued to receive public assistance and I still felt embarrassed by it. The unkind treatment and humiliation from HRS caseworkers added insult to injury and further multiplied my shame. When I (finally) graduated with my Bachelor's degree in 1997, I found a job as a special education teacher in a middle school. The job met many financial needs but was wholly unfulfilling; I knew I was meant for more. However, when I expressed my discontent to others, I was met with comments such as, "You should be grateful you even have a job," and "You're a single mother, don't rock the boat by trying to do more than you already are."

Even though this "advice" was well-intentioned, I knew it was wrong and it was at this point that I decided to allow myself to consider what I really wanted to do with my life and career. From childhood, I'd loved reading and learning. I was drawn to everything written: books, magazines, street signs, anything with words was interesting to me. I also was on a constant hunt for knowledge. Every subject was fascinating to me and I could spend hours getting lost in researching seemingly random topics. I decided that I wanted to surround myself with the ability to read, learn, and lead others to the information they sought. Doing this meant applying to a graduate program in Library and Information Science and relocating back to the university from which I'd transferred when I learned I was pregnant. It also meant figuring out how to fund graduate school.

Once I decided what I wanted to do, it didn't take me long to identify a foundation to apply to, for funding support. The catch was that the only funding they provided was for doctoral studies. I wasn't sure I actually wanted to earn a Ph.D. but I applied anyway. I knew it was a long shot—my cumulative GPA when I finished my undergraduate program was not exactly stellar, and I had no experience in the field of librarianship. I was shocked when I checked the mail a few weeks after applying and found a thick envelope containing details about the program and a letter congratulating me on receiving a fellowship that would pay for me to earn a Master's degree, in addition to a doctorate degree, plus it would provide a stipend!

I remember staring at the information packet, eyes wide in disbelief. I was going to achieve a huge goal that would create amazing opportunities for me and my son and I wasn't going to have to pay a dime! I couldn't wait to share the great news with my parents. My excitement was short-lived, however. While my parents were proud of me, they were very concerned about my ability to raise a child and manage school without their help. To be clear, they did not think I could manage both successfully. To be even more clear, they thought it was a horrible idea that shouldn't even be attempted, as the university I was returning to was eight hours away from them. Even though they offered to raise him while I pursued my educational dreams, I was devastated. Realizing that my parents thought I was incapable of raising my child without their assistance shook me to my core. Even worse, I started wondering, *What if they're . . . right?*

The next few weeks saw my father resigned to (but unhappy about) the fact that my son and I would move out and move on to the next chapter of our lives. My mother, however, did not give up easily. Every few days she would launch into a conversation about what a bad idea my leaving was. She told me I wasn't thinking clearly, that I was being selfish, and that I wasn't putting my son's needs first. When she wasn't berating my decision, she was icing me out with silent treatment.

A few days before I was to participate in the new fellows' orientation, the seeds of doubt that had been planted started growing aggressively. I'd been a "good girl" who hated disappointing my parents and the guilt of upsetting them, even as a young adult, was just too much to bear. With a heavy heart and tears streaming down my face, I called the director of the fellowship program to decline the fellowship. The moment the director answered the phone, I began sobbing and breathlessly choked out my story.

I explained how it was a mistake to have accepted the fellowship, that I wouldn't have any help and I couldn't be a good mom. while going to school away from family, and that it wasn't an option for me to leave my son with my parents. When I finished bawling and blathering, there was nothing but silence on the phone. I assumed that my unexpected outburst had caused her to hang up mid-meltdown and I envisioned her already scanning the waitlist for a name to replace mine. Then she spoke. Even now, over twenty years after the conversation occurred, I still remember her calm, matter-of-fact tone and exact words: "I don't know what is going on and why you would let someone tell you what you are capable of, but we'll figure that out together because I am not letting you pass up this opportunity. I expect to see you at the orientation on Friday."

I'm still not sure why, but those words were a much-needed wake up call. I still had a bad case of the "what ifs," I was still worried about disappointing my parents, and still feared failure. But suddenly, after one brief phone conversation with someone I'd never met in person, I had a renewed sense of belief in myself and I knew that even if things didn't work out, I owed it to myself and my son to at least *try*.

In August 1999, my son and I made the 450-mile trip from Fort Lauderdale, Florida to Tallahassee, Florida. My parents did not, as I'd feared, disown me or crumble under the weight of disappointment. In fact, they became fully supportive, even excited for the new adventure we were starting and drove with us to help us get settled in our apartment. In December 2000, I earned my Master's degree in Library and Information Science and in May 2006, I earned my Doctorate in the same field of study. When my name was called at the graduation ceremony, my mother, who I came to understand had never meant to hurt or discourage me, only protect her daughter and grandson from imagined dangers, reflexively yelled out, "Now that's what I'm talking about!" to the delight of the hundreds of people in attendance.

While I would not willingly endure again the pain of being rejected by my son's father, the difficulty of being a very young single mother, the humiliating situations that accompanied being part of the welfare system, or the gut-wrenching anxiety that came with my concern about going against my parents' wishes, I know without a single doubt that all of these things have ultimately been used for my benefit and God's glory. I am an award-winning professor, I have had opportunities to use my experiences to assist many of my students and colleagues with their personal and professional struggles and difficult decisions, and it turns out that I didn't damage my son—he is an amazing young man with a Master's degree, a lucrative career, and a family of his own. My journey to and through the Ph.D. was long and filled with numerous challenges and each one of them was worth it and necessary to move me toward being the person I was meant to become!

TODD MILLER
Tuscon, AZ

*A Reunion of Friendship*

I REMEMBER THAT DAY in August when my long-lost friend Maurice and his companion, Niko, showed up at my home as planned. A hot breeze was blowing in Arizona that evening, and the sound of my angel chimes swinging in the distant olive tree was the background music as I approached his car with open arms and a big smile to welcome a dear ol' friend who had come to visit, after a long absence.

As my friend pulled himself from his silver Volvo, a man of skin and bones, ashen complexion and an unsteady gait reached out to me, to receive a welcoming hug. I silently thought in a calm, clear way, *Has he come here to die?* I am good at maintaining a poker face in such situations, but I have to admit I was taken aback when I first saw him. We hugged with a powerful "I've missed you" embrace.

Now it was time for Maurice's companion to make his presence known. Niko barked loudly demanding a salutation as well! I rushed to Niko to give him a big hug, too! After twelve years this Schnauzer and I were still buddies and I loved seeing the excitement in his hair covered eyes as he greeted me. I have to say he is one the most adorable Schnauzers I've ever encountered and to this day, he still looks like a fluffy cute stuffed animal at the ripe old age of fourteen.

Now my attention was back to Maurice. I held his arm and led him inside to my living room/office/kitchen which would become his and Niko's new home for the next several months.

Maurice and I had reconnected months back when I first started my most current life work adventure. One of the exercises required of me was to reach out and make amends with anyone that I felt I could have possibly hurt, disappointed or even abandoned in the past. I would then proceed to apologize and ask for forgiveness which would benefit me by releasing any guilt I may be feeling with that person. This in return would help neutralize any negative energy and clear the air between us. It was and still is my goal to live a more positive and successful life without negative feelings prancing around in my energy field. Practicing forgiveness is a daily practice for me. One of my daily spiritual mantras is the ho'oponopono. This beautiful ancient Hawaiian practice of forgiveness functions as both a communication concept for reconciliation and a tool for restoring self-love and balance.

Maurice was one of the people that I wanted to make amends with. Life happened, we lost contact and I missed him dearly. Unbeknownst to me, when I reached out, he had suffered huge financial loss due to the pandemic. Maurice was rendered homeless and surfing one couch and unstable homestead after another. All of this while simultaneously experiencing a near life- threatening gall bladder infection which led to hospitalizations and a long period of recovery.

My dear friend was at his wits end. When he arrived at my home, he had no money, a car that needed a lot of maintenance, and he was now suffering from a mystery illness which drained his energy, clouded his mind and emaciated his body.

"When it rains, it pours!" No one Maurice knew had the time, patience and the know-how to help him with his current health and financial crisis. He needed a place of stability and peace to rest and heal, both mentally, physically and financially. God knew exactly who to send him to, evidently, I fit the bill.

I had just successfully launched my own real estate business and was in my last couple of weeks of my Dream Builder Life Coaching course with Laura Walker, learning how to bridge, build and manifest the life I chose to live. I was in a really great space mentally and emotionally so I was in a position to help my friend tackle his problems head on.

I soon learned that it was possible to assist in the manifestation for other's lives when in alignment with the Universal Energies of Love and Light. I've been known to move mountains when I get involved with a project and with my newfound skills and knowledge of manifesting, I held a firm belief that miracles were on the horizon.

Due to mental fog caused by his mysterious illness, Maurice had never finished his application for his unemployment/pandemic financial assistance, after losing all of his jobs. God was looking out for him and he had a caseworker do more than her job required, to help get him qualified on her end, now she just needed a year and a half of weekly paperwork processed to help recuperate payments owed to him and he had a deadline of two weeks, before his case would close.

I was very busy running my own business but with faith and confidence in myself and with the support of my Angels and Creator, I believed I could pull off the filling out, scanning and uploading of one hundred plus pages to the Unemployment online platform, in time. With his permission, I was able to gain access to all the communications with his caseworker and basically assume his identity, to get the job done. During this process, Maurice sometimes slept for days on end, affected by his illness.

On days that I would be running my business (working from home), Maurice would be laying on my couch with his eyes closed, three feet away, and he would have a smile on his face as he and I would listen to Mary Morrissey's inspirational lesson of the week. I could tell the audios were inspiring him to get better by raising his vibration—a beautiful side effect of listening to Mary's audios.

One day, after a battery of tests, his doctor called and told me to get him to the hospital ASAP. He was finally diagnosed with a serious fungal infection, valley fever, that affects the lungs and other parts of the body, including the brain. The doctor said he needed acute hospitalization and treatment right away. After weeks of using my couch as a hospital bed, we were off the hospital for a week or more stay.

Maurice had been helping as much as he could with the manual filling out of the paperwork between ER visits and exhaustion. But now it was up to me to get him across the finish line as I had a week's deadline to submit all the documentation, all while continuing to run my business, simultaneously. I wasn't sure how much money he would receive when everything was uploaded and processed, but I kept visualizing him with enough money to give him a fresh start in life and I kept seeing him fully recovered from his infection.

Two days before the deadline and countless emails and phone calls later, everything was uploaded and confirmed with the Unemployment agency. What a relief! Now we just had to wait to see what the financial outcome would be. After eight days in the hospital, Maurice was released back into my care. Two days later, I logged into his bank account, and I excitedly announced to him, "You have $8,000 in your account!" The next day I logged in I excitedly announced, "You have $13,000 in your account!" Over the next couple of days, I was soon to discover, my efforts, manifested a total of $19,997.00 into his bank account! Talk about feeling overjoyed and relieved for my dear friend. He had transformed from being jobless, homeless and broke to having the financial ability to start his life afresh post pandemic and illness.

I have to write more about Niko and his role throughout the whole ordeal. He is such a beautiful, amazing dog that I truly believe holds some sort of magical "puppy powers" with the ability to heal others, just by being in their presence. I witnessed the tangible comfort and healing he provided Maurice throughout his whole ordeal.

When it was all said and done, I never thought that I could handle another person, plus their faithful companion, living with me in the small home I rented. What is amazing about the journey is that it never felt hard or difficult. I was determined that my friend was going to be more than okay. I wanted him to be well and live life abundantly!

I am grateful that the Spirit allowed me to assist my dear friend when he was in need. I feel God called me to perform a duty He knew I was capable of handling, and I learned more about myself and the loyalty I hold toward those I care about. With help from the Creator and my Angels, plus the skills I learned through my life coaching I felt at peace, calm, and strong throughout the whole process.

Maurice stayed with me a little while longer and would not leave my side when I contracted COVID-19, with severe symptoms. He stayed to make sure I was okay and looked after. Now that the tables were turned, and I was sick, it was clear the comfort

I felt knowing that someone was there for me. Maurice was able to return the favor and help me when I was very ill for several weeks. Remarkably, he never became infected himself.

I am happy to report that Maurice and Niko now have a secure home to live. All the repairs needed for his car were completed and that Volvo is back in "tip top" shape. Money is flowing in once again and he is fully recovered from his infection. Our recent life experiences together have rekindled our friendship and created a deeper appreciation for life and those that experience it with us. I feel privileged and honored to have the opportunity to demonstrate to Maurice what having a true friend is really like. A true friend will always have your back no matter what. I wouldn't have had the opportunity to demonstrate and carry out these acts of kindness and caring for another human being if I had never picked up the phone that day and said "I'm sorry, please forgive me" to a dear ol' friend. I am grateful to have had a reunion of friendship.

ANAMARI PEREZ
Nomad

## *The Seahorse Miracle*

A YEAR AGO, I was in the best shape in my life, I woke at 3:30am to go to the gym, had a full day of lectures in occupational therapy program, went on a three to four mile walk with my dog daily, and I would work doubles on the weekend stretching people, all while feeling full of energy. I really felt as if I was living in a dream AND it was sustainable. Then all hell broke loose for me.

My precious cat, Steve, got sick and needed two surgeries back-to-back costing $20,000, causing much financial and emotional upheaval. Soon after, my car was involved in two accidents within the same month, through no fault of my own. A family member had a stroke which was shocking and my ex-boyfriend was living on my couch until he could afford to move out. Long story short, I felt like I was drowning, and I didn't know how to pick myself back up.

I fell into a rut; it was as if I had given up completely! I was ordering DoorDash almost every night and only had enough energy to go to work. At this point of my journey with my Occupational Therapy education, I had moved to Northern California and was working full time as an intern at an inpatient rehab facility. After work, I would go home and watch Netflix until I fell asleep. This self-sabotaging pattern lasted for a whole year.

Fast forward to my present life, I live in beautiful Seattle. As I write this short story, I am working as an intern at an outpatient hand clinic. I feel confident, grounded, and clear on who I am while feeling a sense of peace in the decisions I make on a daily basis. This is possible for you too, and I want to share what worked for me so in the event anyone could use some hope, encouragement or help to get unstuck. This is the journey of how I got to this amazing place of confidence, calm and successful thinking.

One day, I simply decided that I didn't want to be the person that only has the energy to go to work and then is too drained to pursue anything else that matters to him/her. I paused and I seriously asked myself what I wanted for my life outside of business and career. I blueprinted what I would love my life to look like *in vast detail*! What would I absolutely love my health, spiritual well-being, relationships, and the way I impact and make a difference to others to look like? After getting clear on what I really desired, I started to notice that I began to have more gut feelings pulling me toward things that I wanted or didn't want.

I then began to shift my perspective towards being in the moment, one day at a time and I began to truly embrace what I wanted to create and be who I wanted to be . . . one day at a time. I was on a wonderful adventure! I felt like I was the author of my life for the first time. I started my mornings envisioning exactly how I wanted the day to go. I let my thoughts go crazy and I would go through different scenarios of how I truly desired the day to go and how I would feel as I would be doing the things I was daydreaming about. I would go all out during this process and use *all* five senses as I cultivated what my dream day will look like.

After doing that for a few minutes, letting my mind run free, I would then write down three things that stuck out the most to me that I would feel really good about, after envisioning them. As the day went on, I started noticing and feeling more of my gut feelings signaling me in my action steps and they were getting stronger. I noticed the more consistent I was with my morning visioning, it began to become very clear what my longings and discontents were and how they would start pulling me closer or further away from what I truly wanted for my life. I began to realize the more that I followed my longings, the more I started to notice positive changes in my life and different opportunities seemed to fall into my lap, effortlessly. I was awake and aware and it was easy to decide to continue listening and following these gut feelings and stop fighting them especially in the moments when I was tired or after a hard day.

The days I showed up and completed my three morning tasks, even if I felt at my absolute worst, the craziest things would happen to me. Not long ago, after a rough day at work, I was walking to my car and I took a moment to pause and take stock of the thoughts in my head. *Oh my back hurts so much, my feet, urgh, I just want to go home and lay in bed with my heated blanket and just be done for the day. Hold up, this morning you told yourself that you were going to go to the gym and do cardio after work! You even packed all your gym clothes, everything is already with you,* my head voice replied, *But my bed sounds so nice.* My gut rebutted, *You know you are going to wake up and feel like a failure and sell-out, if you don't go. Why don't you show up and see what happens. Just show up!* I considered, *Okay, I can do that, . . .* I stopped arguing with my internal dialogue and acknowledged my gut was pulling me to go, so I decided to go for it, what did I have to lose?

As I walked into the gym, I noticed a refrigerator full of bright yellow energy drinks. "I'll take one of those!," I told the woman at the check-in counter. I put the drink up to my mouth, *mmmm delicious, okay I'm ready.* Immediately, I plopped on the mat and grabbed a foam roller to stretch out my back. As I closed my eyes, I felt something wet brush against the side of my cheek. My eyes were wide open, I looked to my right and there was an adorable yellow lab rolling next to me asking for pets. I chuckled to myself, how lucky was I to have found a pet-friendly gym.

I then started my work out, I looked around and to my surprise I looked up and locked eyes with this gorgeous, bearded man and I chuckled again noticing how we were wearing the same burgundy color pants and white tops. *Well, he's nice to look at, I shall be quite entertained during this shoulder workout,* I whispered to myself. I finished my routine and I saw all the cardio machines were taken. Damn! The voices in my head started speaking louder. *Oh no, now what? Well, I do have that membership at "LA fitness" still active. Maybe I'll just show up there and see how it goes, I'm feeling pretty good! I'm not ready to go home just yet, I'm feeling more energized.* I am surprised at how much my thoughts have shifted since getting off work.

I went to "LA fitness." I did my cardio and then I noticed how there was a SPROUTS grocery store next door. *Hmmmmm, I do need more rice to last me for my meals this week, I'll just stop in there really quickly.* As I walked up to the cashier, I noticed this little old woman with six gallon jugs of water in her cart. I thought to myself, *I'll stand in that line, it should be quick.* As I stood a few feet away from the woman and the cashier waiting my turn, I scrolled aimlessly on my phone. After a moment, I looked up, thinking, *this is taking longer than normal.* The woman was having trouble paying the $7.56. She went through one card, the balance came out to $3.28, second card, balance was $1.16.

As I watched this play out, I noticed my body swaying from side to side and I heard the competing voices in my head shouting, *Offer to pay for her water. Oh no, that would be so rude, you are just being inpatient. It would be a kind gesture. What if she's offended?*

I felt frozen, I didn't know what to do. I heard another voice say *she is going through her change now, speak up!* By now, I had started to recognize this pulling feeling, I took a deep breath and spoke up. "Excuse me, ma'am, I have an extra dollar you are more than welcome to have." The little old woman looked at me and her eyes started to well up. She said "thank you so much, times are rough now, you know?" I handed her the dollar and she gave it to the clerk and looked back at me. "You know, the water isn't even for me, I am one of seven people left in the country that breeds and raises sea horses. The water is for their tanks." My cheeks started to hurt from smiling at how adorable and quirky this woman was.

My heart feels full, and I feel so grateful for how appreciative this woman was for receiving a dollar. I am grateful for listening to the pulling of my intuition and I feel so happy that the universe aligned me and this woman to be in the same place at the same time. As I walked away, I am reminded how simple human kindness can make such an impact in other people's lives, as well as my own. I am reminded to slow down and to cherish the little things in life and realize how fortunate I am to design and live a life that is truly meaningful to me. It takes just three minutes in the morning to dream, and then observe how much your life can change.

CYNTHIA PORTER
Spring, TX

## *Empty Nesting is Not Always Pretty*

As I walk Ozzie, my English bulldog, near the lake by our new condo, I stop and close my eyes to keep the tears from coming AGAIN! I am a fifty-three-year-old mother of two boys and a wife of a retired military fighter pilot, who now flies for a major airline. Having gotten married at twenty-four, I have been a military wife and mother for most of my life.

I am now faced with the reality of losing my fulltime mother status, I am riddled with anxiety. Quite frankly I am pissed and angry! There are no more baseball games or practices, book clubs, family dinners or wine with friends. I am literally lost in this new life of mine and beyond sad, lonely and a bit depressed. Where did all that time go? I didn't want my life to change! How dare my boys grow up and move far away from me? I love my husband but he and everyone else always knew where my life started and ended—that was with my boys. My world is completely blown up and I literally feel like I am learning to walk again!

My oldest child lives in Southern California and is finishing his business degree. He moved to the West Coast to play college baseball and did very well until COVID-19 hit. As you can imagine, living in California was difficult . . . they had a restrictive lockdown for a very long time. There came a point that he eventually chose to leave the sport he loved and get his degree completed so he could commence his adulting adventure. We are very close, we talk on the phone every day, sometimes multiple times a day. I am damn proud of my relationship with him, and I don't ever apologize for it.

When my first born was in high school, his usual breakfast was five egg burritos every morning to start the day's thirty-five hundred calorie diet. He had to keep weight on to stay competitive for his college catching career. All meals were at home Sunday through Thursday to help maintain this in a healthy way and it also created precious family time. That could be difficult to create with everyone going different directions.

My youngest son is five and a half years younger than his brother, but he was very much following in his older brother's footsteps. He followed the same regimen as his brother in his aspirations for baseball. However, Covid squashed those dreams as he was offered a spot on a Southern California University team as well, but the roster was locked down. He didn't want to waste time, after all, no one knew how long Covid was going to stick around. So, he chose to give up baseball and just go to college. He is now very happy as a member of the Phi Kappa Psi Fraternity and is entering his second year of college. We always thought he would be a Frat Boy! I definitely call him that. My relationship with him is different from his older brother. I don't always talk to him every day, but he knows he is loved and thought about just as much. He's just more independent and I am so proud of that!

I often ask my husband why my boys grew up and wanted to move so far away from me? Why couldn't they stick around and go to college locally? I have a few friends with that luxury, and it just does not feel fair! I am Italian and grew up with my Italian grandparents. My uncles didn't go far! Some never left at all! Why couldn't that be me? I know, I know! I raised them to be independent and they felt confident starting their new life away from me, but damn it, it just wasn't fair.

So, I thought and prayed about how I was going to navigate my new normal. Of course, I still have my job and my husband and my Ozzie, but what will fulfill me and make me feel whole again? I have no trouble being alone, I have been doing it for all of my married life as my husband's military career took him away quite often. But I always had the kids to keep me busy. I always had the friends that stemmed from the kids to fulfill my "me" time. I am literally starting from scratch, and I had to find something that would give me a new lease on life. The bottom of that wine glass was just not giving me the answers I needed, so that's when I decided that I needed some guidance.

Starting my "Life Coach Land," a twelve-week course is exactly what I needed to change my life. Can I put this bluntly? This shit really works! I started meditating, manifesting and affirming what I would love my life to look like and things started changing!

Let's be honest, I was in a new city that I didn't choose, and my husband was traveling a bunch and I had to find a way to fulfill my soul and give some purpose to my life. I joined a book club and met a new friend that I adore and am learning so much from, as our connection is through empty nesting. I have wonderful people that live in our new condo that have shown so much kindness and support. I have joined the Homeowner Association (HOA) and have started helping renovate the interior of our building and it looks amazing (if I do say so myself).

I travel, travel, travel because I fly for free! I have decided to do all the things that I couldn't because I was raising kids and they had activities and all the attendant responsibilities that came with that.

In this ongoing journey to find what I would love my life to look like, I have discovered many things about myself, as well. The good and not so good, but knowing I have the ability to change those behaviors and thoughts has made my life fuller and more purposeful. Every day I send gratitude to the universe and thank God for all of my blessings. I have recently had an opportunity to stay in Southern California for an extended amount of time. This allows me the ability to spend quality time with my family, my son and friends.

To sum this up, don't walk, but *run* to the life that you would love to live. We are in an abundant universe and it is there for the taking! Don't let excuses or fear stop you from having the best life you can have. Believe me when I say that it goes by in a flash and things can change so quickly! Go out there and grab the happiness you deserve!

**WENDY REVELL**
Southlake, TX

# *My Identity*

I DON'T KNOW if anyone ever told you but there's a thief that comes to steal your identity from the very beginning of your life. My first encounter with this thief was when I came into agreement with a lie that was whispered in my ear.

You see, when I was a young girl, my mom would tell me the story of how my daddy had wanted a little boy. By the time my sister came around, he was so in love with me that he wanted another little girl, but what penetrated my heart *and* stuck was the phrase that he wanted a little "boy." I took that lie and I protected it and allowed it to grow and tell me who I was.

Of course, my daddy really loved me and it was the lie that I was believing that told me I wasn't good enough. This moment gave birth to many moments of pain over the years and when I was a little older I believed the second lie that would bring pain and confusion to my life (purity is outdated and stupid). What I had been taught as a child was that purity, in relation to my body, was because God did not want for me to get hurt and that some of the consequences could be extremely painful, not just for me, but also for those who loved me. I was taught that sexually transmitted diseases and getting pregnant out of wedlock were some of our worst fears as Christians.

I felt as though I could handle the "not getting hurt" part. Walls up, now I would be able to distance myself or disconnect from my partners emotionally and use my sexuality as a tool to get what I wanted, whether that was to feed my insecurities for a night or to use my body to gain popularity and approval. I thought that I was very powerful by being able to separate my feelings from my actions. Oh, what lies I believed! *I'm a strong woman*, I would tell myself.

My first encounter with sex was when I was sixteen. I was not in love. I was using my sexuality to keep a boy interested. This was my first experience that would define my attitude towards sex. Once I had given away my virginity, I felt there was no need to save myself anymore. Sex became a game. At the time I fully believed that if two people could mutually use each other for satisfaction, then there was no harm being done. By the time I was a senior I had had multiple partners and I was desperate for genuine connection. I thought I had found it in a young man, whom I met at a party. Spoiler alert—not necessarily the ideal place for a soulmate.

I did what I normally did, which was try to capture his attention with my body. The sex worked for a short time, but his eyes were always wandering. Devotion wasn't his strong suit. I thought I could change him. This was my first co-dependent, abusive relationship (emotionally, verbally, physically). Although I thought that I could control the emotions that come along with sex, I was deceived—I could not. Why not? Because, frankly, that's not how God designed us. It will take me years to figure this out. I thought we were in love; I became pregnant at nineteen. I then married the father of my child and we divorced a year later, after months of unending drama.

I went into a downward spiral and began to use drugs heavily and experiment sexually. I abandoned my two year old daughter and she went to live with my parents. Over the next three years, I was seeking to find what had eluded me for all those years. The desire to be loved was so strong, so I went back to what I had learned in high school, which was to use my body as a tool to attract boys and girls to fill the void in my life. I met my second baby daddy at a club, again, not the place for a soulmate. He was supposed to be a one-night stand, that segued into short term boyfriend that eventually led into a friend-with-benefits situation, for five years.

Sheesh! I moved homes and was slowing down my single scene, when I became pregnant with my son. I knew that I did not want to make this situation worse by marrying the father for the wrong reasons, like I had previously done. I believed that at the very least the seven years of journeying had made me a smidge wiser. You don't want to compound your bad choices by doing the wrong thing long-term. So, I decided to raise my two children on my own with my parents' involvement. Yes, my parents are saints and deserve all their flowers!

After my son was born, I began to reflect on how I had been raised and wondered where I had gone wrong? The direction that my life was headed was not what I wanted for my future or my children. So, I had an honest conversation with myself, *I haven't been acting like I knew who I was created to be*. A level of conviction settled in that I hadn't felt in a long while. Lies began to disappear and I could sense hope on the horizon. I started going to church again. I'm an all or nothing kind of girl, so I dove in headfirst and immediately signed up for three bible studies. My parents said they would watch the kids as long as I was pursuing my faith.

*Up until now*, I knew a lot about Jesus but it was mostly religion. Now I was seeking a relationship. Something that had eluded my heart for all these years. I allowed God to reveal to me who he created me to be and show me my identity in Him. People like to label us, sometimes that can become your identity. We must only listen to His voice. He is the only one with the authority to define His creation. So now, I know who I am and *whose* I am. I am a woman of worth, I am fearless, I am a daughter of the King. He set me back on my feet and gave me clear direction. Freedom was beginning, for me.

Then, totally unexpectedly, I met a young man in a bible study. We became fast friends. The more I found out about him, the more I was intrigued. Something was very different about this guy. He was smart and funny, very handsome, kind and he was a virgin (um, excuse me?). Honestly, now, I have never met anyone that was over twenty, good-looking who was still a virgin. To say he was a unicorn to me, is an understatement. I remember asking him why he hadn't slept with anyone, and he told me that it wasn't because he didn't have opportunity, but it was because he wanted to save himself for his wife because she was a treasure and he wanted to be able to give himself completely to her as a gift, on their wedding night. I must confess I was a little stunned at first and thought he was a little out there.

A few months later I really began to dig deep into my faith. I started to see the reason and truth in my friend's statement. I started seeing things with new eyes. I began to hunger for purity. I decided that that's the kind of relationship I wanted to start afresh, with someone. To not have any physical attachments to cloud my judgment. A year or so after we became friends, I began to date the man from the bible study and when he decided to court me, he sent me flowers to let me know that he was in pursuit of me. I had never been pursued! I began to praise God! Wow what a gift! Side note: that's literally what his name meant—"Gift from God." God provided for me, the girl who had made so many mistakes, had two children out of wedlock and yet He had saved his very best for me. I was this man's gift. He had been waiting for me. I couldn't believe it!

I was his and he was mine. The stresses of past partners for me disappeared. There was no comparison to our wedding night. It was beautiful. God gave me the love of my life whom I didn't think I deserved but God saw me for who I am and thought I did. My life now looks nothing like my former life when I didn't know who I was. I now have best friends who are the exes of my exes. We all share several half siblings. I know it sounds strange, but with God all things are possible, and our children have one big happy family. My oldest daughter calls it a bush not a tree. I have been redeemed in so many ways, it just took me a while to come out of agreement with the lies and accept who I TRULY was all along. I found that Jesus loved me just the way I am. Scars and all.

What I have learned is that my God is faithful and He loves to redeem! It's never too late to change and allow Him to restore your identity.

CRYSTAL SCHUDER
Forth Worth, TX

## *A Phone Nudge from Heaven*

MOTHERS ARE A VERY important part of our lives. My mother had epilepsy. When she was eleven years old, she fell on the playground and hit her head. Six months later she started having seizures. This happened in the late 1950's and as you can imagine, back then, they really didn't know how to handle seizures. It was almost like a death sentence in that era.

My mother married and I was born in 1972. She had two children, my brother and I. My father left in the late 70's. She was a single parent raising two small children and living with a disability; because of this she was unemployable. I remember when I was around seven years old, I witnessed her having a seizure. I was so scared! I was this little girl, and I had no idea what was wrong with my mom. Luckily my grandparents lived close by, and I called them and they came to help us. There were so many times that my mother needed to go to the hospital due to her seizures. It seemed that they were out of control. Over the years, as I got older, I learned how to help my mom when she did go into a seizure. When I was sixteen. my grandmother gave me one of her extra cars, so we finally had a car in the family. I was of driving age and now had a car, so my grandmother no longer had to take us everywhere we needed to go. My mom was a great parent. She didn't have a lot of money but the love that she showered my brother and I was way more valuable than any money she could have ever given us.

The year 1995 was the best and worst year I have ever experienced. I married in June of 1995. A few weeks after I was married, I found out I was expecting my first child. I was so excited and overjoyed . . . we were thrilled! Tragically, just six weeks after my wedding, my mother passed away in July of 1995, from a seizure which segued into a heart attack, taking her life. I remember my brother calling me at work and saying, "I need to speak to Crystal" I said, "This is Crystal!" He was trying so hard to be calm, but panic was permeating his voice as he spoke. "I really need you to come home right now" he said with masked emotion. I responded, "If mom has had a seizure just take her to the hospital." He was insistent I leave and come to my mom's house. I told him, "Okay, I'll leave right now and meet you there at our apartment, that we grew up in."

I was walking to my car when something inside me told me I needed to turn around and call my husband. I knew to listen to that voice, so I called my husband and let him know that something had happened to my mom. I told him that I was not sure what had happened, but my brother Clint had called, and he needed me to meet him there. I was pregnant and my mind was racing. If she needed physical help, I was not in a position to lift her. I told my husband I need him to meet me there.

At the time, I worked on the West side of Fort Worth, and I had to drive to Burleson. That was the fastest I've ever driven to Burleson. When I finally made it to the entrance of the apartments, I saw my husband waiting for me. He wanted me to be prepared for what I was about to see. He let me know that my mother had passed away and there were several emergency vehicles in the parking lot.

When one passes away at home, the authorities must investigate to rule out any criminal activity.

I believe that day my intuition spoke to me. It nudged me to go back and call my husband so he would be there with me, on the hardest day of my life. When we have reflected on that time in our lives, my brother and I feel like God was there for us, in preparing us for the loss of our mother. The night before my mother passed away, we spoke on the phone for over two hours. She was so excited for the grandchild that was coming. The grandchild that she was never able to meet, she even bought a few outfits without even knowing the gender of the baby. I'm so grateful for my mom. The hardship that we had growing up and the love that she gave to all the people around her was a true inspiration and I will forever be grateful. I was eventually blessed with four children of my own. Unfortunately, they never got to meet her, but they know she is their special angel watching over them.

I was twenty-two when my mother passed away. I did not have my mother there for me when my first child was born. I could not call her for any advice, but I know that she is my special angel watching over my family and for that I will always feel her love around me.

JACKIE SCOTT
Sunbury, PA

# *Cyrus's Spaghetti Lesson*

"I'm running late again. I'll be there around 4:45pm, to pick Cyrus up. Urgh . . . I'm sorry I have to go. My phone is ringing again." Glancing at the dashboard of the F150 work truck, I accepted the call. *Thank goodness it was a short call and simple fix,* I thought. *I'm exhausted, traffic has been a nightmare today and the route home took almost twice as long, as usual.* I dropped my truck off at home then hopped in my car and was racing off again, to pick up my rambunctious three-year-old son.

"Hey honey!" I said as he ran to give me a hug. I started strapping him up in the car seat and he began telling me about all the toys he played with, what he saw in his favorite TV show that he wants now, oh and "Mommy, are we going to the park?" he continued.

"I'm sorry Cyrus. We can't go today, we'll go tomorrow. We're running out of time. It's already getting late." I said as we pulled into the parking spot outside of our house. We had finally arrived home but there was little time to play and certainly no time to go to the park. I was already thinking of making dinner, my phone was still ringing with employees needing support and guidance from an extended night job that was happening in the field, and then it was going to be our nightly bedtime routine of brushing teeth, bath time and then bedtime stories. *I'm definitely going to bed when he does tonight!* I thought to myself.

"Okay honey, I'll be in the kitchen. I love you" I said as I glanced over at Cyrus. "What are you doing!? Absolutely NO! Please get off the cat tower now, before you hurt yourself or something else!" I yelled, mortified.

"It's okay Mommy, I'll be careful" he said as he jumped fearlessly from the top of the tower to the recliner, then over the side table to the couch. Surprisingly, he wasn't hurt, and nothing was broken.

"Cyrus, I do not want to see that again!" I said sternly, but also kind of impressed at his agility, although I wouldn't encourage that right this moment. I paused waiting for his response. "Cyrus? Do you understand? Absolutely no more climbing and jumping in the living room! That is for cats, not little boys to play on."

He looked at me sweetly with those innocent eyes and said "okay mommy" and shrugged it off, moving onto the next thing.

I began walking to the kitchen and wondered what extracurricular he needed to be enrolled in so he would stop doing parkour in the living room. *I'll save that thought for later consideration*, I thought to myself.

A few minutes later, Cyrus began riding his big wheel in the living room, then into the kitchen, crashing into or running over anything that was in his path and back again. My mind was still bouncing around from one task to the next. Between conversations with him, managing evening work phone calls, and trying to decide what to cook for dinner, we were quickly running out of daylight. "Spaghetti it is!" I said out loud to myself, thinking, it's quick, easy, and difficult to mess up.

I went to the refrigerator and grabbed the ground beef, turned around quickly, knocked a plastic children's bowl off the counter from an earlier snack and watched as dry cereal went flying everywhere. "Ooookay" I said, taking a deep breath. I put the ground beef on the counter, then quickly began to pick up the cereal. Noticing the cats needed to be fed, I asked Cyrus. "Hey baby, can you please feed the cats?"

"Oh yeah, sure mommy." He said excitedly riding into the kitchen again. That's the one household contribution he has mastered rather quickly, and he does it well.

I washed my hands and went back to the ground beef to start breaking it up and to season it but then I realized I was trying to make dinner without even turning the stove on.

"Urgh Jackie, you're such a dumb, dumb . . . ," I said quietly to myself, but obviously not quietly enough. Cyrus was back on his Harley-Davidson big wheel, cruising into the kitchen and halting next to the chair. He looked at me matter-of-factly and instructed, "You can't say that! That's a bad word!"

I was genuinely confused. I wasn't sure what I had just said but I was pretty sure I didn't swear. Although, I had already moved on to the next thought so it's possible I suppose. "What can't I say?" I asked while looking at him.

"You can't say 'dumb, dumb.' That's a bad word." He elaborated casually as he started hiding toys under his motorcycle seat cover.

"Oh honey, that's not a bad word. I can say that."

He stopped what he was doing and gave me a perplexed look "So it's a nice word, then?"

I paused the conversation for a second to think before speaking. "Well, no. Okay, I see where you're going with this," I said. "You are right . . . it's not a nice word and I probably should not be saying that. I am sorry." I replied not only to him, but also to myself. "I should be much nicer with the words I use and to myself, thank you, Cyrus."

He understood and was satisfied with the results. It was over and he started pedaling away as fast as he had come in, crashing into the kitchen table and chairs once again, then spinning around quickly and heading back off into the living room.

I just stood there reflecting. What exactly just happened here? Usually, I am a very positive person but I didn't realize just how much negative self-talk I actually did have. Consciously, I was excellent with the thoughts and words I chose to entertain, but subconsciously I was much more critical, judgmental, and a lot harder on myself than I realized . . . and he saw that.

It was not lost on me either that Cyrus chose the word "nice" instead of "good." Had he questioned whether it was a "good" word, I probably would have gone off on a tangent explaining that it was neutral or something like that, not really bad per se, but not good either, but he didn't. He chose the word "nice" instead.

That slight change of word completely changed the trajectory of our conversation and no, I absolutely did not want him thinking it was okay to talk to himself that way. I wouldn't let him go around calling other people names and I don't do that either, but why did I think it was okay to treat myself that way?

I've always tried to teach him awareness and respect for himself and others, but I didn't realize where I was lacking, with my own self talk. That was the example I was setting for him, but it was time for a change. He made that clear in his childlike quip that was *very* aware.

This was not one of those major shifts that completely turned my life around, in an instance. I have worked on myself personally and professionally but this was a more subtle shift. One that could have easily been missed.

*Up until now*, I was so focused on the BIG things. The things that were in the forefront of my mind and in my awareness, but I realize now that there's always a next level I could achieve no matter how skilled I think I've become with any habits, tasks, or goals. This was honing a skill that required a certain level of self-awareness and finesse, to move to the next level of personal development.

This may not have been a huge shift that everyone would notice, especially not immediately, but it absolutely changes how I will continue to treat and talk to myself. It changes what my son observes, how he learns to treat himself, how he'll choose to be an example, and how he'll choose to teach and guide others in the future.

That evening I finished dinner for the both of us, and let the rest of the tension from the day slip away. I am so grateful for the level of introspection I'm able to receive through a slight nudge from a three-year-old and our spaghetti dinner.

Finally feeling relieved, with our plates and drinks on the table I called Cyrus back into the kitchen. I knelt down to his level, looked him in the eye and said, "Thank you for all your help honey." Then I wrapped my arms around him in a great big bear hug.

ANGIE SINN
Mansfield, TX

## *Choices*

Being the only girl in a family from a small town in East Texas, getting married and starting a family was a top priority. I had a happy childhood, and one might say my mother's family was one of the last of the "greats" from the Great Depression. My grandfather was in World War I and was the youngest of thirteen children. He was a romantic and wrote love letters to my grandmother while away. I can honestly say I never saw them apart from each other. Some of my best times were spent at their home, playing cards with my grandfather, playing sports with my cousins over the holidays, and jumping on our neighbor friends' trampoline. My grandparents never missed a football game or special event of any of their eight grandchildren. Our entire family lived in the same town and we were all close to each other, as our lives and life events intertwined and connected us deeply. My parents were a younger version of my grandparents. I learned what "family" means from my parents but witnessed it playing out in the lives of my relatives from my mother's side of the family.

After high school, I went to college. It was the best time in life for me and I ended up doing pretty well. I made some of my best friends while there and met my future husband. We dated all four years of college, and I married my college sweetheart, right after graduation. His new job post-graduation had us relocating to Phoenix, AZ. He started the day after we returned from our honeymoon. I remember my parents and visiting cousins taking videos of our family opening all our wedding gifts to show us, because the movers had come to pack us for the move to Arizona while we were on our honeymoon. After the move, we settled into our life in Arizona. It was just the two of us and our dog, Abby, eighteen hours away from family and friends, but we were excited about the new adventures life presented. After a year, we had an opportunity to move back to Dallas, TX for my husband to take over a sales territory. We enjoyed Phoenix but missed our family, so we jumped at the chance to move back home!

Three years after our marriage in 1997, I gave birth to our handsome first son and life just got better every day. We were so happy and things just seemed to flow with the addition of our son to our little family. My husband was selling dental implants and decided to go to dental school in 1998. He did very well and graduated in 2002. Even though he was now a dentist, we went through many challenging experiences from 2000–2002 that greatly impacted our marriage.

In 2003, we built a brand-new dental practice from the ground up. Later that same year, our second son was born. We were thrilled and the boys adored each other. We had fun and life got busier! My husband and I, together, decided I would leave my job in pharmaceuticals in order to learn every position in our dental practice and manage it until we found help we could trust. I would work part-time in our practice and raise our children to school age, then go back to work full-time.

Over the years, my husband and I continued to face challenges that we just couldn't seem to overcome, and we ended up getting divorced in 2009, just after our fifteen-year anniversary. Never in my wildest dreams would I have imagined myself getting a divorce. I honestly didn't even believe in it. I was raised thinking I could get through anything when it came to family. I always loved my husband and wanted it to last.

Sometimes in life, you reach a point where you discover you have to make a healthy decision that is hard but is for the best for your family. That's what I did. We struggled with issues on and off for seven years, separating toward the end. I had an epiphany toward the end, after a friend shared a bible verse with me that suggested God might be trying to get my attention to let him handle my husband instead of me. I was hopeful and we later took a family trip to Las Vegas. We let the boys swim, went to dinner, and later we went to see Cirque du Soleil. A week later, my marriage began to unravel.

Being a newly single parent brought all the challenges one would imagine. Just the simple fact that my children had to leave me the first, third, and fifth weekend of every month to be with someone I despised, at the time, was like death to me. The impact on my young teenager and toddler was almost unbearable to watch. I will say that I always wanted my kids to have a strong relationship with their father, and I always followed through on allowing him his time with them, regardless of my personal feelings for him, at that time. In the beginning years, it was difficult because my ex and I were not at peace, plus most of our friends quit spending time with us since we were no longer a couple. But, amazingly, life goes on. You do what you have to, to survive. I always had supportive parents by my side. I am so very grateful for this because without them, I would not have made it through, in the positive way that I have. I also maintained a healthy relationship with my in-laws.

Struggle, I did. But I did everything in my power to stabilize my boys' lives and they remain my priority . . . and to this day, I count them as my biggest accomplishment.

I entered the real estate industry in 2012 and went into business development in the title industry. With help, I have been able to support myself, build a career, and my family along the way. I credit God first. I am grateful for the time I had with my husband and in my marriage, as some people never get that opportunity to forgive and shift perception. I realize that my sons and I are stronger today, for all we have gone through. My experiences allowed me to gain independence and confidence, as well as the ability and empathy to help others going through their own challenging times. I'm now in my tenth year in title and I've grown and developed personally and professionally. I enjoy helping others succeed as well.

Fast forward to today, my ex and I are better friends than we ever have been. He remarried and found sobriety and I joke that his wife likes me better than him. We all get along and spend time together with our kids. We are great co-parents. My oldest son is married, and I gained an amazing daughter-in-law. My youngest son is thriving and will attend college in the fall. We're not perfect, but we love our family and the choice to be together on this journey called life.

KEN STIVER, M.D.
Bellingham, WA

## *Migraine, A Lesson to Remember*

WHEN I WAS YOUNG, I remember growing up always feeling sure of myself and safe with my family, our neighborhood, and my friends. I had an older brother and sister, and we grew close, in response to our sometimes demanding and difficult father. He could say things that hurt your feelings and then quickly forget them as if they never happened. My Mom wrote it off as the meningitis he had had in the military, as she was told it might "change" him. It was never talked about. He was a strict disciplinarian, hardworking and always took care of the family. He was active in the Catholic church and prominent in our local parish. I stayed out of trouble by listening to his discussions with my brother through the forced air heat ducts we had. I learned what not to do.

I remember my first headaches in elementary school. I would see a twinkling blind spot in my vision. When it faded, it was followed by a splitting one-sided headache, nausea and vomiting. The pain usually lasted six or eight hours and occurred every couple of months. Once I knew I had to live with it, I usually got upset and cried over the virtual hell I would have to live through. Each year I would have to train my new teacher that when I said I needed to go home I meant it—there was vomit on the floor to show my sincerity. The headaches were always the same and they were miserable. While in pain, I frequently thought that if they were more frequent, I would rather be dead. The headaches consumed me and I didn't have the headache, the headache had me. I lay in bed and suffered through it and wanted to be left alone. I never complained when they ended, and I was never taken to a doctor or had a specific diagnosis. None of this troubled me at the time.

The headaches got a little less frequent as I grew older. My father died suddenly and unexpectedly, on a Sunday, in the fall of 1962. My brother and sister went off to college, and our family went from a house of five to just my mother and I. It was a shock, and none of the adults in my life, including my mother, ever spoke about death and loss with me. I went on about my business. Much later, and in retrospect I realized that my headaches ceased after his death.

As a teenager, I met a resident physician who lived in our neighborhood. I used to talk with him when I babysat his two sons. His wife was the TV weather lady, and when he was on call he needed to have a babysitter already in their home. Another long(ish) story would describe my decision to go to Medical School while I was in high school. I breezed through undergrad, was at great pains to meet all the requirements, went through med school and graduated while working summers in hospitals and thinking little of what I was privileged to do. I had a pager, worked in surgery as a tech, was learning new things every day, and felt valued and content.

While I was in med school, I learned in a lecture that I had classic migraines, and although less sophisticated than current treatment, the treatment was relatively effective. It was a simple diagnosis to make.

I was not sure what I wanted to do after Medical School, as I went in wanting to be a surgeon. Clinical training in surgery and witnessing what older physicians were subjected to during their Residencies gave me pause—their journey was unnecessarily demeaning and demoralizing, and this was kept alive by a power structure of seniority. I couldn't and wouldn't subject myself to that and felt adrift after years of education. I met a Cuban child psychoanalyst and my focus changed. I skated through the last year of Med school by telling everyone I was going to be a psychiatrist, so all expectations of performance would be dropped as the training docs thought they would be wasting their time, with me. After my internship year in Denver, I took a year of what was then called general practice training, and Family Practice was in its infancy.

I worked as a General Practitioner (GP) for several years at small rural hospital south of Eureka, CA, with older senior physicians who set bones, did surgery and delivered babies, amongst other things. There were no specialists, and severely ill or injured patients were transferred up to Eureka. The GP's took turns seeing the patients who came to the "Emergency Room" and often it was a frightening place to be, due to lack of specialists and general surgeons competent in trauma care. My friend from Denver and I did a little of everything, worked hard, where on call all the time, and after two years and the first California Malpractice Insurance Crisis, we closed our practice as we were both insolvent and could no longer afford to run it.

I started working in ER's locally, which was a new thing, as I needed to make at least a little money to survive. ER residencies were a new thing, and many GP's transitioned to staffing ER's.

I became partners with several other physicians, and we started the ER at St. Joseph's Hospital in Eureka. We all studied, learned and became Board Certified in Emergency Medicine. I sat on my committees, loved bioethics, and grew with the community and demands of this new specialty. I was adept at treating difficult patients, and my partners often grabbed the charts of patients who had more objective problems and less chaotic lives. I enjoyed my talents, but often felt resentment for the extra time and care I gave some people. Several times during the twenty-six years I did this, I found myself wondering why I continued. The specialty was increasingly concerned with billing and collections. I had to find new meaning for what I was doing. Some of my patients helped me in this pursuit. I remember one in particular:

I picked up the chart of the patient in Bed one. The name seemed familiar, I walked into the room and introduced myself. The patient wanted to know if I remembered her. I said yes, as I have seen her many times for recurrent migraines in the past, but not recently. She said "I want to thank you for saving my life." I said "Thank you for saying that, what have you been doing since I last saw you?" She told me that she was much better, her migraines were less severe and infrequent. She said she knew she was a difficult patient, and that I was the only physician who she felt cared about her. She said that she remembered me telling her I thought most of her migraines were the result of a problem, not the problem itself. She had been through in depth therapy, had discovered repressed feelings and made progress in her self-image. She said she had a moderate headache on this day and was glad to see me again. I treated her appropriately, she felt better, thanked me several times more, and left.

Throughout the rest of my shift, I thought about what she had said to me. I realized that life had brought us together again. *What if I wasn't here today, I would have never heard those words.* Her feelings, and my care would still exist in time and space. Nothing could ever erase them and she was grateful. I have thought about this off and on for some time, as it had a profound effect on me at that time in my life, as I was going through a period of professional struggle.

At various subsequent times, I have continued to have thoughts of this event. When one does good, it is sent out and "is." If it is not received or appreciated, it "is." It only needs someone to do it and then it is created. It is not contingent on understanding, acceptance, consent or anything else. And it can be done so easily and in so many ways.

Know that "goodness is," just as love, beauty, and peace are. It is eternal in time and space, and is carried by the sender and receiver. It is there at all times and in all places. All we need to do is let go of the impediments to it manifesting—hurry, need, guilt, greed, anger, judgment etc. My understanding of this has grown over the years and continues to grow. Please allow goodness to manifest itself. You can feel it. Peace be with you.

RENEE TOWNSEND
Grapevine, TX

## *Rising Above*

IT WAS STRANGE. On paper, it looked like I had everything a high school girl could dream of: a starting position on Varsity, a handsome boyfriend, and several friends. But, in reality, I was miserable. I never thought I would experience bullying firsthand. I could expect some natural gossip between girls, but I never expected to truly be bullied. I especially did not expect the lengths one would go to sabotage my life.

It all started in middle school when I was the new girl, and the attention was placed on me and not her. She and I were both great athletes and could have been great friends. We were the same position in our sport, shared friends, and had similar interests. Unfortunately, these similarities are what formed our rivalry. I didn't want or ask for this rivalry, but she didn't know how to share the spotlight. If the spotlight wasn't on her, it couldn't be on anyone else. It was just in her nature. I was comfortable sharing the spotlight because we were both excellent players. She was bold, outspoken, and aggressive. On the other hand, I was timid, softspoken, and non-combative. We were polar opposites with the same goal in mind. Our goal was to be the best player in our position.

My rival constantly tried to overshadow me in middle school, and I, being the new kid, allowed it to happen out of fear of conflict and wanting to fit in. Our middle school coaches adored her, so, I had no choice but to live in her shadow in 7th and 8th grade. She was favored by the coaches, not because she was the better player, but because her dad would brown nose the coaches by bringing them gifts, sitting in on our practices, and playing middle school politics. I knew something didn't make sense because outside of school, I earned a spot on one of the best club teams in the state. While she played for a sub-par club team that her dad created because she couldn't compete on an elite club level. Her dad simply was unable to handle his daughter being second to anyone.

As I entered my freshman year of high school, I decided that I was tired of being overlooked—it was my turn to have the spotlight. I knew my skill set and what I brought to the table, and it was time for me to be properly recognized. She and I went head-to-head in high school tryouts. We were both competing for the same spot on Junior Varsity. My rival was very used to getting what she wanted, and her dad would do anything to help her succeed. The politics carried over into high school, as her dad tried to intimidate me during tryouts and spread lies about me to the Varsity head coach to make me look like a bad person. He viewed me as a threat to his daughter's success. I should have been shocked by these actions. But the sad thing was I had already been conditioned to this type of behavior in middle school, and I knew their tactics.

After a fierce competition, the coaches could select only one of us for the team—and it was me! My days of being timid and quiet were over. I knew I deserved to be there, and all my efforts had finally been rewarded. My patience and commitment paid off. To the disappointment of my rival and her dad, their politics wouldn't work this time. I felt like things were finally fair. My freshman year of high school was a dream. As a starting player, I had an incredible season on Junior Varsity, and our team went undefeated, 33-0. I truly felt on top of the world. All the stars were finally aligning. But unfortunately, it wasn't to last. My rival and her dad made sure of it.

After the season, the pair of them made it their mission to get the Junior Varsity and Varsity coaches fired. They still could not come to terms with the fact that I was chosen over her. Surely, there had to be something wrong with the coaches in their mind. So, they rallied other freshmen players and their parents against the respected coaches. Together, they contrived a lengthy grievance letter that they had an attorney draft. They presented this to the school superintendent, ultimately leading to the resignation of these coaches who had been there for roughly eighteen years. It was all, "he said, she said," and the coaches didn't have the time and energy to get into a legal battle, so they went their separate ways. It was suspicious because the girls that filed the grievance letter never had those coaches as *their* coaches since they were on the freshmen team with a different coach. My rival was thrilled because she had a new opportunity to beat me, and she felt confident she would.

This brings us to my sophomore year of high school. There were brand new coaches. Nobody's positions were guaranteed from the year before, and everyone had to prove themselves again for a spot on the team. The tensions were high. My rival was ready to bring her best to prove that freshman year was a fluke and that she was the better player. I was ready to prove that I could beat her regardless of who the coaches were. Despite her and her dad's best efforts, the results stayed the same. I was selected for Varsity, and she was selected for Junior Varsity. However, little did I know that this would be the beginning of the end of my athletic career.

Our rivalry reached a boiling point, and nothing could prepare me for what was about to ensue. Throughout my sophomore year on Varsity, my rival began to build an army of haters consisting of two of her best friends, my fellow teammates. She could not stand me living the life she wanted for herself. These girls were intimidating and cruel. To this day, I still have not met anyone worse than those girls. The bullying started right off the bat of sophomore year. It began with typical girl drama, gossiping behind my back and laughing at me. I thought to myself, *this is temporary and surely won't last forever. I can handle this.* Boy, was I wrong!

This emotional torture continued and quickly escalated. I noticed I was growing insecure mentally and emotionally. My best friends/teammates were aware of the psychological torture, and rather than stick up for me; they decided to turn on me and join the growing army of haters. No one wanted to take my side even though they knew the other girls were in the wrong. They didn't want to make themselves victims of bullying, and I didn't blame them. Those girls were scary.

I felt ostracized, and it was drastically affecting my confidence as an athlete and young girl. Every time I walked into the gym for practice, I was overwhelmed with anxiety. The sport that once came so easy and effortless to me felt like an impossible challenge. I found myself making mistakes or ruining a drill, which was uncharacteristic, and I felt as if my skill level was regressing. I had little to no confidence left. And to be a great athlete, you must be confident in yourself and your skills to perform at a high level. That part of me was now broken. I grew frustrated, and depressed, and to make matters worse, I no longer had anyone to turn to within the sports program. I wanted to be done.

It's wild to think about the mental toll bullying can have on a person. Throughout that Varsity season, I lost ten pounds due to depression, the loss of my best friends, and I lost my love of the game I had played since the age of seven. To make matters even worse, the new Varsity coach had turned out to be a bully herself, and her coaching style was incredibly damaging to my psyche. Everywhere I turned, I was getting judged, criticized, and tormented. My mind couldn't take it anymore, and it boiled down to making one of my life's most difficult decisions. After ten years of incredible memories, accomplishments, and friendships, I decided to hang it up forever. This decision did not come easily, but I decided that my mental health was more important. There was no way I could endure the relational bullying for two more years, especially after losing the support of my best friends. I had lost my love and passion for the sport. I was crushed and defeated.

The day I quit will always live with me. It was a very surreal day because I had lost half of my identity. My entire life up until that point had revolved around the sport. I remember walking out of my coach's office, crying my eyes out and wondering where to go next. I entered the locker room to grab all my belongings. As I was leaving, my former teammates came in, and the army of haters started giggling and whispering. The last thing I heard before I shut the door was, "She's gone!" and an eruption of laughter, which confirmed that I had made the right decision to leave that toxic environment and escape the abuse once and for all.

Unfortunately, the bullying continued to worsen during the last two years of high school. I had naively thought that quitting and leaving the sport behind would stop the bullying because without me there anymore, my rival could finally be the "best." I guess it just wasn't enough, as she was still bent on vengeance. Every day was a struggle because I knew I would be pointed at, laughed at, or talked about. I couldn't even show my face at a school event without being negatively talked about.

Students who never met or spoke to me joined this army of haters because they were friends with the ring leaders. So naturally, they believed I was some loser they should also hate. It felt like half of my classmates were against me, and none of them took the time to get to know me or hear my story. One of the worst episodes of bullying was the vandalizing of my car and home when I was out of the country on vacation with my family. My elderly grandma was house sitting and walked outside to discover my car, mailbox, and front porch covered in eggs, sardines, syrup, condoms, dog poop, pizza, ranch dressing, Vienna sausages, and toilet paper. I was utterly shocked when my grandma called to tell me, and I couldn't comprehend why the bullying was worsening.

The active bullying and acts to antagonize me continued for the perpetrator's own enjoyment and entertainment. I thought to myself, "I've given everything to my rival. I gave her my varsity position. I gave her my friends; what more could she want from me?" The answer came and it was devastating. She took the first boy I ever loved.

The constant months of bullying had taken its toll on my relationship with my boyfriend and we broke up in my junior year. About one week after the breakup, my rival slept with my ex-boyfriend to spite me; to deeply hurt me. She made sure to go around the school and let everyone know about being intimate with him because she hated me. Obviously, I was devastated to hear this, and I became unhinged. It was seriously the worst emotional pain I had felt in my entire life. My first love was sleeping with the girl who ruined my high school life. It was a very dark time emotionally. Honestly, the thing that killed me the most was all the betrayals I had experienced in a short time. I was in so much [emotional] pain.

I share this story because I know that I'm not the only one that has had this experience. There are people that experience way worse in high school or life outside of high school for that matter. Every day, there are people experiencing pain and suffering and they feel like it may never get better.

Well, I'm here to tell you that life does get better, and the very pain you are feeling is shaping you into the person you are meant to be. That might be hard to understand . . . especially if you are in the middle of a similar bullying or betrayal situation, as you read this.

I learned through my journey, that without all the trauma, I would not be nearly as mature, successful, and independent as I am today. I learned so many important life lessons at such a young age. I grew tremendously. Although I will never forget the trauma I went through in high school, I discovered that in order to heal fully, you must be willing to forgive. One of the best friends that I had lost due to betrayal ended up coming back to me during my senior year and asking for forgiveness for what she had done, and we are still friends to this day.

After high school, I shifted all my energy and efforts into academics. My dream had been for a very long time to go to Texas A&M University, and I accomplished that goal. I was able to rediscover my identity in college. I found who I was at my core outside of the sport that was once my identity. That person is kind, forgiving, motivated, resilient, and incredibly strong.

Today, I make it a point to go out of my way to look out for that person who may be struggling to fit in or who may be getting made fun of, anyone who looks like they might need a hand to hold onto. I do this because I wish someone would have done it for me in high school. I never want to make someone feel the way I was made to feel, and I will do anything in my power to prevent that same sort of pain. At the end of the day, life is too short not to be kind. Everyone deserves to be treated with respect and kindness. After all, it is the golden rule to "treat others how you wish to be treated."

KEENAN WHITAKER
Huntsville, TX

## *In the Blink of An Eye*

I WANTED TO DO THIS STORY, but things kept getting in the way, with work, changing fields, money issues and new beginnings. But God continued to bring Laura back around to remind me that my story can help so many out there who need that push to continue and not give up no matter how rainy it may seem right now. It can turn around in the blink of an eye. If you give up and give in, then you let the devil win, but God, our God is bigger than the devil and anything he can throw our way. I am sitting in my truck right now, contemplating how far back to go with this tale, what to include and exclude, because there is so much to say.

I'm going to go back eleven years, to when I started working in Residential Treatment Centers (ROTCs). I was referred to this field by my younger brother who said, "You have always been great with kids, this job is for you." I applied and got the job in New Ulm, Texas. Soon thereafter, I began working long hours and days at a time, with troubled kids who had very intense behaviors. I eventually moved into supervisory roles there.

Over the years I have seen just about everything you can imagine, working with special needs minors in a group home situation.

Kids have seriously tried to hurt me in all kinds of ways. Hitting, kicking, biting, spitting, stabbing, to mention but a few. Nevertheless, I continued working with them because the transformation in a child from their first day to the end, when they are discharged, is very heartwarming and feels like a job well done. I ended up getting my Licensed Child Care Administrator License (LCCA), while I was there.

I stayed at my first facility for four years before changing to a better opportunity in Huntsville, Texas. I made the change because there were many open promises that weren't fulfilled. I began to excel at the facility in Huntsville and moved up to supervisory roles, but once again, I continued to have open promises not fulfilled and there always seemed to be an excuse as to why. I would be told that I wouldn't be getting the promotion because there was no one to replace me or "sometimes it seems like you don't want to be here," etc. But, in the same breath I would always be assured that I was one of the best to have come through the facility. So, which was it?

I have had a lot of hurt and disappointment over the years. More from the administration of the facilities than the kids themselves. Children were easy to deal with because once you showed them the love, respect, and the compassion they have always wanted, then they respect you and have good behavior when you are with them. It opens a door so they can talk to you about their problems, before things escalate. You see it from working with them and it facilitates the de-escalation of the problem.

Fast forward seven years. I continued to experience hurt and broken promises throughout the years. I was demoted when I contracted COVID-19 and refused to come back to the facility while sick. They said that it was because of some of the things I said, "they don't care about us since they are bringing kids in without testing them [for Covid]" and more. I was merely voicing health and safety concerns, not bad mouthing the organization, for the sake of it. Then they got in a bind and wanted me to take over a house that had a reputation for having out of hand behavior (from the kids) for a year and half. I considered it and let them know my salary request. They wouldn't meet the salary I requested, so I declined.

Shortly after, I met Laura Walker on Facebook. Somehow, we had been following each other for years. I needed some counseling because I knew I was sinking in all areas of my life. Reaching out to Laura was one of the best decisions of my life. During this time, her training began to help me see things differently and work on my relationship with God, which helped me work better and not get so stressed at work with the lies and BS I felt I was constantly being fed. I began to apply for jobs and have interviews during this time. Funny thing, is every time I had an interview, Laura always said, "You won't get it, that's not for you." I started thinking to myself *who is this lady and why is she so "against" me?* She continued saying that and also saying, "There's three things at your current job you have to work on before leaving." This went on and on, leaving me confused, frustrated and scratching my head, but I continued working with her and it was helping. We ended our course two to three months later and one day, I told my dad it was time for me to switch fields. I figured he would say "Keep looking in the field you're in" like he always did. To my surprise, he didn't, he said "Yes, it is, go get your Commercial Driver's License (CDL)." I started studying here and there for two weeks and went in and got my permit within a few days. I then signed up for a class and it didn't start until the final week of March.

So, I continued working with the kids. I needed three weeks off but figured the admin wouldn't give it to me, as usual. I continued to use Laura's techniques and listened to my wife. I put the application in and boom, I got it. Fast forward, I did three weeks in the class and took my driving part and passed and got my CDL.

I knew it was my way out, but then the devil came back and put an allegation on the house I was working in and as a result I have been off the job with no pay for the last three, going on four months. But God still continued to provide, and I got a CDL job OTR, finished my training weeks early and now I just completed my first week solo and drove all the way to Michigan. The case is almost over at the other job and they will back-pay me for all that time. Look at God! Always working it out for my good, if I just be patient, stay out of the way and let Him work, continue building a relationship with Him.

Not only was I drowning with my work situation, but my marriage was drowning as well. It was definitely my fault, not being the man God has called me to be and being faithful to one woman. Laura's techniques helped me here too. She always said, "Keenan, what do you want?" I can hear her now, to this day. I continued following her techniques and it just seemed like something wasn't right or it just wasn't the marriage for me. But, my wife and I continued living together, growing in our own areas and being there for our wonderful, smart, athletic, handsome boys. We continued being cordial, but it kept seeming like nothing was working. Continued trying by working on myself and building a relationship with God. A lot of the marriage hurt came from work as well because, you spend so much time with your colleagues that one thing can lead to another. But, in the back of my head I could always hear Laura, so I have continued staying in there and not moving out and just letting God work. Once, I went to truck driving school, it opened both our eyes up to miss one another and what we both brought to the relationship outside of the physical, which we weren't having anyway. Once I began driving trucks and the finances improved and I was away from the old job, our relationship began to get stronger.

We are talking on the phone again like when we were dating and not wanting to get off, like high school kids talking for hours.

We still have aways to go, but at least we are on the right path and there is less time to do anything troublesome due to my trucking schedule of running and getting loads done on time. I know the future is bright and I must continue allowing God to use me and build me into who He has always intended me to be. I now strive to be the husband, father, son, entrepreneur, and Godly man that He needs me to be and give Him all the glory and honor that He so deserves.

I don't know who this message might be for, but don't give up, keep pushing, keep climbing. Set aside time to pray daily, even throughout the day. Don't be selfish and pray only for yourself, but also pray for others and even people you don't know. Get in a bible-based church to learn more, give back and for sure give tithe, your 10%, before taxes. Read God's word, do Bible plans and most of all give God all the glory and honor and bring others to know Him. Share your testimony about what He has done for you because we all go through things, not just to go through, but for God to get the glory for what He brought us through and for us to share with others who are going through or going to go through a similar situation. Don't give up and let the devil win, scream right now, "devil get out of here, my God is bigger and greater than you and you can't have me!"

KIRSTEN FAGAN
Semmes, AL

## *Guardian Angels and Facing Fears*

ONE MORNING I got in my car to head to work. It was pitch black out and very quiet. I enjoyed my morning drives to work, as there was hardly anyone on the road and everything was quiet and peaceful. But this day was different.

The day before I had spilled bleach down my leg and burned my skin. In the process it ruined my cell phone. So, while I was waiting for a replacement phone, I grabbed an old phone out of the drawer and began using it. The phone wasn't great, but I figured it would be ok as long as I had something to make calls on. But on this particular day, I would quickly realize how much I needed my phone.

As I began driving, the road was pretty empty, per usual. I always enjoyed cutting across some back roads to get to work quicker. I was getting close to being back on the main road and as I looked up, I saw headlights coming straight towards me. Thoughts ran through my mind . . .

*Are those lights in my lane?*
*That truck is in my lane.*
*He isn't moving back over . . .*

My heart began to race. I knew I had to think fast, or he would slam into my car. He wasn't switching lanes and he wasn't slowing down either. I quickly pulled my car off the road as far as I could but I didn't have enough space for the entire car to be off the road.

It happened so fast. I can still hear the sound of the car crunching and the metal scraping down the driver's side of my car. Glass shattered and I felt sharp pain across my face. I can still hear the glass hitting the seats and the windshield behind me. It felt like slow motion and I felt and heard every bit of it.

Finally, the sound ended. Eerie silence. I looked over my shoulder. I saw red brake lights on a white truck. *They stopped to help me!* I thought, grateful. Then suddenly, the truck engine roared, the brake lights went off, and the driver sped off.

I was left in total silence and was pretty stunned. *What should I do?* I looked over and saw a teenage boy standing in his front yard. As our eyes met, he quickly disappeared back into his house and I was alone again.

*Why did he leave me?* I was alone again, and I felt scared. I reached for my phone and started calling people. I called my husband. No answer, he was a sound sleeper. I called my in-laws who lived nearby, but there was no answer. I knew they were probably sleeping so I quickly tried to call 911. The lady answered and kept saying, "Ma'am, what's the emergency? Ma'am, I can't hear you, your phone keeps breaking up." I finally just hung up the phone in frustration. No one could hear me.

So, I called my parents. Finally, my dad's soothing voice came on the line and he said, "Kirsten, what's wrong?" I said, "Dad, I was hit by a truck." But he couldn't hear me. My phone was breaking up and I quickly went from calmly telling my story to falling apart and crying and yelling into my little old, stand-in phone.

To this day I don't really know what my Dad heard, but he said, "We are on our way."

A short time later a police officer pulled up and he shined his flashlight in my face and asked me if I was okay. I squinted up at him and said, "Not really, your flashlight is blinding me." He quickly moved his light and asked if I could get out of the car and if I could move. I told him I was a bit shaken up and asked him if he could open my door. He paused for a moment . . . "um, you don't have a door handle." He reached in through my broken window and opened my door. I climbed shakily out of the car.

Around that time my parents pulled up, an ambulance came and my dad let me know he was going to go get my husband.

The sun was coming up and I caught sight of my face in the reflection of my unbroken window. I was shocked to see blood running down my face. Up until that moment I had thought I was fine and the only thing that was damaged was my car. I looked at my Mom and remarked, "I'm bleeding."

A lady with the ambulance asked me what I needed and I looked at her. "I have glass in my pants. I need to get it out," I said. Everyone laughed and quickly I was surrounded by blankets so I could get the glass out of my clothes. It was everywhere.

Finally, all the family began pulling up, as we were deciding what to do next. My mom said she would take me to the ER and my Husband and Dad said they would get my car home.

As I started to walk to my mom's car I noticed the window missing out of my car door. That side of the car was flat, the metal was pressing down on my tire, there were no door handles and my windshield was broken. The back seat was filled with broken glass. It was hard to believe I had just been in that car and emerged [relatively] unscathed.

The rescue team began hammering the metal off of my tire so the car could be driven home and I settled into my mom's car with shards of glass in my face but I was filled with gratitude to be alive.

We waited for what seemed like an eternity in the ER, but

finally the doctor came, removed the glass and gave me some medicine to help with the aches and pain. He said, "Young lady you are lucky! You have no severe damage, but you may be sore for a few weeks."

Over the following weeks, maybe even months, I felt nervous to drive my car and I could not bring myself to drive on the road where I had been hit. Anytime I would think about it, the fear would creep in and I would go around the long way. Finally, I realized that if I was to move forward, I would just have to do it.

Mustering up my courage, with my heart in my throat, I turned onto THE ROAD. I didn't want to be there, but I did it anyway. I drove slowly, gripping the wheel tightly. I was waiting for someone to be in my lane and I watched every driveway as I went by, judging just where I could run to and escape.

As I came to the light and turned onto the main road, I realized that it was over. I had faced my fears. Tears came to my eyes as I realized just how grateful I was to be safe and alive. And at that moment I realized I was no longer afraid to drive on the roads I wanted to drive on and I felt like I had received a piece of myself back.

JACKIE SCOTT
Sunbury, AZ

## *Friday's Coffee Revelation*

I WAS AT A CROSSROADS IN MY LIFE. I just wasn't sure what direction I was going to take, where I was headed, or what I was going to do when I got there. I was just leaving the Navy. I always thought I would be what we called a "lifer." That is someone who stays in the military until retirement and makes a career of it. My entire life plan up until I was twenty was to stay in the military, but it wasn't exactly the life I imagined. I felt lost. I felt like I had no control over anything that was happening around me. It felt like a whirlwind of circumstances that's being directed and orchestrated by others and I was just there following along. But you know what the sad part was? I didn't have any clue what the problem was and since I didn't even know that, how was I supposed to change it or find the answer?

I searched and found a new job. This was exactly what I was looking for . . . kind of. There were no weekend work requirements, overtime was optional and there were benefits. This was something quick and easy to transition into and it was a plus that I was going to be working outside. I wouldn't be stuck on a ship or inside a building all day. Although traffic control was definitely not something I ever thought would be in my future, it would be a new experience that I was going to embrace and I was excited.

"Alright! I have an interview!" I said to one of my Navy friends as we swept the hallway. I was no longer on the ship but I was in a Naval facility in Harrisburg. I told him where and what the starting pay was. He looked at me with raised eyebrows. "That's what you want to do?"

"Well, no, it's not exactly my dream job or final destination but it's something different until I figure that out." I explained. I already knew this was going to be one of those "in-between" jobs—the kind you get just to make do and pay bills but you're definitely still looking for something better. I had little to no expectations from this transition, but I did know I was ready for the change.

Four months passed. I was still a crew member at Flagger Force, but I found myself helping newer crew leaders frequently. I called my supervisor. "Okay" I said. "What the heck, send me to class. I might as well move up while I'm here." I became a crew leader, then three months later, I was promoted again to advanced crew leader. I had been with the company eight months, at that point.

It was a beautiful summer day in Pennsylvania with just enough wind and tons of trees to keep it comfortable but I didn't notice and that's usually something I would always appreciate. I was so focused on what I was tired of seeing happen that I couldn't see the forest for the proverbial trees. I've met some amazing people but was so tired of others complaining, or not seeing the support we needed in the field, people blaming or criticizing and gossiping. I saw chaos, confusion and complaints blah blah blah blah blah. This was exhausting and it was getting old. I was starting to be what I was tired of seeing, but I didn't even realize it. You name it and I was probably complaining about it, too. I looked at my coworker and sighed. "You know what, I'm so done. I just don't care anymore." I paused for a few minutes. "I'm going to look for a new job." I said feeling completely defeated. I had all the complaints at the front of my mind and each one of them felt like a huge issue at the time. It's no surprise I can't even remember specifically what I was so concerned about.

He looked at me and said "Honestly, I think you do care. I think you care a lot and that's why these things are bothering you so much. Why don't you apply for the safety committee?"

I wrinkled my nose "The safety committee? I don't know about that." I considered it, "Okay. If nothing else, it'll be a change from being in the field and be a new experience."

Thank God for good conversations and an amazing network of co-workers because that was definitely food for thought. After I digested this new idea and gained some insight, I realized he was right. I did care and I did enjoy the people I was working with and the job itself, but the actions I was about to take wouldn't have reflected that not even in the slightest. It certainly wouldn't make any changes that would help all the issues I was complaining about, so I decided to do something different. I applied for the safety committee position that night. I was interviewed and I accepted the new position.

One Friday morning (during one of the earlier meetings), I poured myself a cup of coffee, got out a notepad and pen, then sat down. Work was starting to feel a little more balanced and I was actually feeling excited again. I had an idea and jotted it down nonchalantly. When there was a pause in the conversation I casually submitted my idea in a "what if we . . ." scenario, not expecting much. The safety manager asked me to elaborate and that's when I got a little more animated. I was excited at the thought of making positive changes. Then I stopped abruptly. I could feel the words getting hung up in my throat. The room was silent. This wasn't stage fright or fear of public speaking. This was a sudden appreciation for something I'd been missing and needing from my working environment, but I hadn't realized it before.

Within seconds, thoughts ran rampantly through my mind. I glanced around the team sitting around the room. *Was everyone here actually listening to my input with honest interest? No one was dismissing me, my ideas, or stifling them with a power trip?* Then I felt a sadness and could feel my eyes starting to well. Shouldn't it be this way all the time . . . ?

*Up until now*, I didn't have a voice, or should I say I wasn't being heard. In that moment I had a newfound power and sense of self. I cleared my throat, shook the thoughts from my head and got back in the moment. I realized just how profoundly my environment can help or hinder my success, but I had the ability to make those changes myself. *Up until now*, I've let the circumstances around me dictate my thoughts and actions but in that moment I felt empowered and realized I could make the necessary changes if that's honestly what I wanted to create in my life.

Now, I know I'm not able to control *all* circumstances but I am in control of where I choose to be, who I choose to be around, what I listen to, and the actions I choose to take. "I just don't care anymore" could not have been further from the truth, but it did require a shift in my perspective. It's not that my complaints for the situations were not valid, but the power and ability I had to effect change was far greater than the problems themselves.

I decided I wanted to be that for other people. I wanted to help them feel empowered to create a change in their outlook on life and their work environment as well. I continued to advance in the company to field specialist and then to area supervisor. I began guiding and coaching others in the field not just with their technical skills and knowledge but with their soft skills and their own personal development as well.

It has been six years since that "a-ha" moment. I've learned to lean into my passion, discovered new interests, and accomplished goals I never would have considered. Knowing that I have the power to change and influence my environment anytime has been one of my most transformational and inspirational experiences. My experience with my career and the people in it, has been full of ups and downs, twists and turns, and many more blessings than I could ever count.

One short sentence from a friend, and one small action step led me on a path of transformation that is substantially more astounding than I could ever have imagined. I now know that no matter what the future holds personally or professionally, I will always have the ability to choose how I feel about it, and the actions I decide to take.

LAURA WALKER
Keller, TX

## *From a Broken Heart to Love on the Eiffel Tower*

As the car raced down the freeway toward the airport, the car tires whirred. They gripped the asphalt road providing a white noise effect filling the space of silence that was proving deafening throughout the cab of the car. This was it . . . our romantic relationship was coming to an end, for now. My heart was broken, hurting, and very heavy. How could this be happening?

Hanson and I met two and a half years earlier. Over the course of our relationship, we shared love, laughter, tears, family activities, fun, holidays, and travels around the world. We weathered COVID-19 together and so much more. Ultimately, the fact that we were on different pages about our relationship and where we wanted it to go brought things to a head. It was now time, after graduating my youngest of four children from high school to figure "me" out.

As we pulled into the airport terminal, a sob welled up in my throat and I choked it back before it escaped my mouth. I quickly wiped away the tear trickling down my cheek, so he didn't see it. *I am not about to let him see me cry,* I told myself defiantly. *No way!*

A mixture of anger, hurt, and courage came over me. I wanted to take our relationship to the next level and get married. He did not. So now it was time to move on and figure it all out. Honoring and respecting his wishes and mine, leaving was the choice I must make for my future, while honoring my core values.

As I entered the Dallas/Fort Worth (DFW) terminal, Hanson walked me in. My heart thudded in my chest. Part of me was ready to run through the Transportation Security Administration (TSA) security away from him and the other part was longing to hear him say, "Babe, I love you, don't leave . . ." But that did not happen. As I headed through TSA, I looked back at him one last time. Staring into his eyes searching for connection, almost begging him to stop me. He did not. I guess that only happens in the movies. I turned and walked away, resolved and stoic.

As I sat on the plane heading to Colorado, my mind wandered, running through all the "what if's?" Pushing those thoughts aside, I deliberately filled my mind with the dreamy adventures planned for Colorado. I ordered a second "Tito's" and soda with extra lime. "Tito's" was going to be my best friend for the next two hours enroute Colorado and I looked forward to the next chapter of life. My eyes were heavy. They closed, and I drifted off into an inflight nap.

Landing in Durango, CO made my heart so happy. Family vacation memories over the years and lots of fun had been had in Durango. The excitement began to build in me about an inspirational and fun Dalai Lama themed Airbnb, booked for a full month! There were so many adventures lined up over the next few weeks; exploring food, white water rafting, riding the Silverton train, ziplining and working with new clients via Zoom, while in the beautiful Southwest Colorado mountain town.

My dear friend Amy had decided to visit from Texas, and we planned a road trip to Telluride, by way of Ouray via the Million

Dollar highway. We planned to just enjoy the gorgeous scenery while noshing on yummy foods and sipping fab wines.

As my month in Colorado went by, I met new people and grew my coaching business in a magical way. I loved meeting new people and learning what made them tick. I ventured out into town in the evenings, and people I met over dinner and around town began to ask, "Where are you going after Colorado?"

Honestly, I had asked myself that very same question! I hadn't really thought about it. But a few days later, I got the answer like a lightning bolt in my soul . . . New York City! It seemed obvious to me! I had always loved New York, so why not?

Without hesitation, I began to identify as, and refer to myself in conversation as a "Citizen of the World." This happened almost daily with new friends I met, explaining when asked, that I planned to travel, work, and have new adventures as I go. As things unfolded, I saw definitively that this journey was going to take me many places over the next twelve months, and I committed to that adventure wholeheartedly with zeal, excitement, and enthusiasm!

After enjoying a very adventurous month in Durango, with weekend visits from Amy and Hanson, I was New York City bound! I love New York; cliche I know, but so true all the same! After Colorado, necessary tweaks were made to the "Citizen of the World" adventure. The decision was made to forgo Airbnbs going forward. "Where would I love to stay?" I asked myself! Midtown, at the stately Warwick was the resounding answer!

After landing at JFK, I was picked up by my amazing client Louise, a New York City native, and her husband Tony. As we spent the afternoon driving through Manhattan, I received the gift of seeing this amazing city through their eyes as if I was on a private tour for hire. We swapped stories and many jokes and laughs. We ended the evening with an amazing al fresco dinner at a quaint, posh Greek cafe off of 55th and then called it a night.

My work was thrilling! New committed and engaged clients were enrolling weekly. I would meet with clients by day via Zoom and gaze out of my twenty fourth floor window over 54th street and 6th Avenue to Radio City Music Hall. The hustle and bustle of the city was spectacular. The energy was positively palatable and invigorating.

Hanson came to visit for the weekend, while I was in New York. He had never visited New York and I could not wait to show him all the sites this amazing city had to offer. What an amazing time we had; Rockefeller Center, the Staten Island Ferry, the One World Memorial, Central Park and more. Seeing this historic city through the wonderment and excitement he felt was a gift!

As our weekend ended, I knew the romantic cord needed to be cut completely. A clean break. I was flying to Rome, Italy in three days and was staying in Europe for a month. I couldn't continue the back and forth, it was too much for my heart knowing we had no real future romantically. It was time to be definitive and create space for my "forever" man to come along.

As we readied for our final day together in New York, once again I found myself sad and broken hearted, our NYC weekend had come to an end, and it was time to part; for good.

As we were about to head out for breakfast, something snapped in me, and I began to cry. All of a sudden, it all came pouring out, without control. The words tumbled out of my mouth like lava flow—everything that my heart wanted but couldn't have with Hanson up until now.

I shared with him my dreams of what I really wanted in a man, in a marriage. I shared dreams about my future and business and supporting people who were hurting and struggling. I had a vision of a marriage that I firmly believed God had planted in my heart and I told Hanson exactly what I would love my life to look like personally and professionally.

I paced the hotel like a crazed lunatic. Back and forth, back and forth. The room that had served as my home and office for the past three weeks was now my safe space to unload my deepest feelings to Hanson while he sat there and listened wide eyed, through my rant. It was as if I was walking on hot coals. Brisk steps were punctuated with my solid and steady words. Those words held my truth, my vision of what I would love my life TO BE.

Eventually . . . the emotions leveled, the intensity subsided a bit and when I met with his eyes he looked directly into me and asked, "Is that what you want? What you really want?"

"Yes!" I answered, "and if you're not 'it,' then this is the part where you go home and you no longer get to come visit me anymore. I have to make space for the right man in my life."

The silence was deafening. But the answer, his reply, was swift and steady, "That's exactly what I want, too!"

I was stunned. I could not believe what I was hearing. The voice in my head was chattering at me like an incessant nag, "See now you've done it! You've effed it all up, again, Laura! You are going to Europe, NOW WHAT? You always make rash irresponsible decisions" . . . blah blah blah . . . *Up Until Now*.

My heart felt a small leap of hope. But I was leaving for the other side of the world in seventy hours and I would be gone at least for a month, if not longer. So now I knew I had to trust the process. I had to breathe and proceed with my plans and see where this newfound unity of vision would take our relationship. My excitement to head to Europe was overriding any preoccupation I had about this unexpected turn of relational events. I embraced the excitement and distraction.

Rome, Italy. Amazing! It was so much fun traveling and taking all my clients with me! How miraculous and amazing that I could unfold my computer, turn it on and meet with clients all over the world from anywhere in the world! I was one blessed girl to work in this capacity and boy, did I ever utilize that advantage in the summer of 2021!

As my adventures in Rome unfolded, I found a beautiful rhythm in the days that passed. The majority of my clients were back in the United States, so I would sleep in until 1:00pm and then start Zoom sessions around 4:00pm, Rome time, after popping out to the local cafe, Gran Caffè del Passeggero, that was right around the corner from my hotel. Some afternoons I'd take the fifteen-minute walk to the Colosseum, have a glass of prosecco, and then head back to my hotel with a to-go of grilled chicken and veggies to snack on in between client sessions.

I loved it! I would see clients via Zoom Monday to Thursday finishing up by looking out the window to see the sunrise over the beautiful ancient city of Roma. Weekends were dedicated to exploring everything I could! My first Saturday in Rome, I signed up for a walking food tour in the ancient part of Rome, "Trastevere." The bustling, windy cobbled roads were alive with the youth of the city and we popped in and out of several eateries, sampling the foods and wines of the town where Julius Caesar once resided.

As the days passed, Hanson and I spent hours talking and reconnecting . . . it was magical. It was as if we were completely rediscovering each other. It felt unifying, vulnerable and real. By the second week, whenever my phone would ring and I would see Hanson's name on my caller ID, I would be filled with a youthful excitement. We would chat about anything and everything. On one occasion he said, "Babe, I want to come see you, may I come during the last seven—ten days that you are there? I'm coming and I'm coming with a ring!"

My heart leapt in my chest. *Did he just say what I think he said?* I asked in my mind. *Don't dare ask him to repeat it,* I cautioned myself, continued to trust the process. I was thrilled, happy, cautious, and scared simultaneously! I had trusted the process, stayed the course, and not only was I having the adventure of the lifetime personally and professionally, now it seemed like life would finally be heading in a direction I had dreamt of, with the man I truly loved.

Hanson kept his word; flights were booked and I was over the moon that he was coming to Europe. What would this new adventure bring?

I counted down the days with anxious excitement. The beautiful flow that I had created in my schedule was continuously shared with Hanson and my kids with the miracle of Facetime. And then d-day came; Hanson was arriving! I felt like a sixteen-year-old schoolgirl! I finished my final client's session at 5:00am and Hanson's car from the airport was scheduled to arrive at 8:30am. The sun was beginning to come up, peeking through pink and orange clouds, shining it's beautiful August light on the new day I had anxiously been waiting on to arrive. I was exhausted, excited, happy, emotional, nervous, and ready—all at the same time! It was a mixed bag in the best possible way.

When the black Mercedes pulled up to the hotel, I was seated in the Star Hotel lobby sipping a third green tea to stay awake. I saw my Hanson exit the car and walk through the automatic doors and into the hotel lobby with the morning sun streaming in. His handsome chiseled features were such a joyful sight to see. At that moment, I knew it was real. I knew this was a defining moment and I was giddy with excitement for the next ten days to unfold.

We soon hit our stride and began to decide where we wanted to go and what we wanted to see, while we were in Europe together. I had paused all my client sessions for vacation break and we were free to go anywhere we wanted! As we pondered and plotted, the list of stops began to grow.

A car was rented for our adventures and off we went! Tuscany was up first with stops in Florence and Firenze. Then South to the gorgeous coastal towns of Sorrento, Naples, Pompeii, the Amalfi

Coast, the Isle of Capri and Positano. AMAZING! Then Hanson said, "Let's go to Paris!" and who was I to say no? Flights were purchased and we were on our way to Paris, France. It was a whirlwind and a dream, simultaneously!

The next morning, opening my eyes in a gorgeous boutique hotel in Paris, France, I knew that things were unique. I sensed the energy in our room and had a knowing that today was going to be special.

We quickly decided to take the short fifteen-minute walk to the Eiffel Tower. There was a chill in the air and a light drizzle that stopped as quickly as it would start. As we ascended the Eiffel Tower to the second level, families with kids off from school on break were chatting and laughing in French.

We explored the second level taking in the 360-degree views of the stunning city. It was remarkable and my excitement levels were off-the-charts. As we walked through the museum and shop area, the wafting aroma of freshly baked crepes lured us to explore. We quickly ordered a Nutella filled crepe with whipped cream and a glass of champagne. When in Paris, right? Hanson took my hand and suggested we go out to the observation deck. My heart skipped a beat.

Hanson gently led me to a bench. We sat down and suddenly it was as if the space emptied. It seemed no one was around yet, just moments before, it had been replete with young lovers, rambunctious children, and amazed tourists. The sky was cloudy and there was a light drizzle, the view of magnificent Paris all around us was unobstructed.

Then Hanson spoke. It was as if his voice was the only voice in the physical realm. "Babe. You know I love you. I want to spend my life with you, I want to marry you and take care of you mentally, physically, emotionally, spiritually, and financially for the rest of your life!"

And then a box emerged. *Was this happening??? Here??? Oh my gosh!!!* The beautiful smooth blue box showcased a gorgeous marquis cut diamond solitaire that sparkled brilliantly in the sunlight that was now peeking through the clouds. My head was spinning and now he is down on one knee. My heart was pounding in my chest . . . *THIS IS HAPPENING!*

"YES, YES of course my Lovey! Of course, I will marry you!" I replied without hesitation! We laughed and kissed and I could hardly walk. It was as if I was drunk, giddy and over the moon simultaneously. I looked at the gorgeous marquis solitaire ring on the third finger of my left hand and clung to Hanson, kissing him all over his handsome face. It happened. It really happened in a very magical and special way.

Even to this day, I pinch myself to make sure this life I live is real. That this dream is not some apparition that could disappear. This is my dream life . . . I created it with God's vision for my life planted deeply in my heart. I changed my thinking and changed my life. I am beyond grateful!

# FEATURED CONTRIBUTORS

# *Matt Alexander*

Matt is a tenured marketing and advertising professional with agency and client-side experience, focused on driving new revenue into businesses. Industry experience includes dentistry, DSO/DPO space, Ophthalmology & Optometry, banking, mortgage, consumer products, and loyalty incentive solutions.

Currently, he's the Director of Marketing for a multi-practice, multi-specialty eye care group in Fort Worth, TX focused on growing new patient volume and engaging current patients through integrated marketing campaigns.

Previously, Matt worked for two dental service organizations as a Marketing Director serving over two hundred dental offices across the nation. Matt also integrated new practices into the organizations by assessing their needs and creating strategies to increase revenue and new patient numbers. He also managed the marketing strategy and execution for forty-seven offices in Texas and Arizona, specializing in multi-office locations and de novos.

Matt started his marketing career on the agency side which included managing a small boutique agency in the medical field (dental, ophthalmology, and optometry practices) where he created and managed strategic integrated campaigns to increase revenue and drive new patients into their practices. He's managed websites, performed SEO, SEM, PPC, email drip campaigns, SM and marketing tactics, as well as training the frontline.

Graduating from Texas Christian University with a Bachelor of Science in Communications with an emphasis in media management and production, he has clearly made his mark. Go Frogs!

When Matt isn't working, he loves traveling around the state of Texas for the best tacos and scuba diving locations.

# *Dani Atkins*

Hailing from Grand Rapids, MI, Dani Atkins is an Action-Charged Empowerment coach, specializing in ballroom dance, multi-style choreography, and Pilates. She is the creator of the "Eight Week Hero Challenge," author of "No Cape Necessary," and designs courses, journals, and other resources to help others take action and level-up their self-confidence.

As a dance professional, she has had the honor of winning multiple championship titles in American Smooth and Specialty Styles, she has performed and trained internationally, choreographed for and danced on national television, entertained and assisted in multiple charity events, raising millions of dollars for the fight against breast cancer, and earned her Masters Examiners Certification in American Ballroom.

When not in the studio or lost deep in projects on the computer, she enjoys playing piano, composing music, painting, golfing, reading, baking, traveling, hiking, visiting with friends and family, and finding new ways to expand her physical and artistic horizons.

She is enthused to be included in "Up Until Now," having greatly benefited from that exact phrase herself—it's the perfect reminder that amazing life shifts can occur at any moment, even up until now, if we are paying attention and choose to follow the subtle but "sparkling feelings" of our intuition.

## Loralee Broer

Loralee Broer is a multilingual, international traveler and passionate child advocate. She studied in Rome, Italy and received her Master's degree in International Public Affairs. She also has her Bachelor's in International Relations and Associate's in International Trade.

Loralee was born in Huron, South Dakota on a farm, but when she was eight years old her family moved to Eastern Europe. Growing up in Kosovo and Macedonia gave her a unique and dynamic upbringing and she had traveled over most of Europe by the time she was nineteen.

When she was a young teenager, she visited an orphanage and fell in love with the children. That is when her passion for advocating and helping children was ignited. She has experience as a court appointed special advocate of abused and neglected children. Her advocacy extended to the medical arena when she was blessed with an extra special son, born with heart defects. For over fifteen years, Loralee has continually studied personal growth and implemented transformational success principles in her own life. Practicing the principles she has learned helped her navigate and overcome some of the most difficult challenges in her life.

Loralee lives in Denver, CO with her two children Gabriel and Katarina. She enjoys hosting dinner parties, dancing, traveling and spending time with her family and friends.

# Maureen Connelly

Maureen Connelly is a registered nurse in Wilmington, Delaware. She has been an educator and caregiver for forty-two years at Christiana Hospital, a large teaching hospital in Delaware.

Maureen has contributed to the nursing profession through a long and very fulfilling career.

Maureen has worked in various medical units throughout her career but her favorite was being an adolescent nurse. Recent endeavors include tutoring nurses that are pursuing their nursing degrees. She wants to emphasize to nurses that they can do anything they put their heart and mind to, as stated in the book "Up Until Now."

When not being a caregiver and educator, Maureen enjoys travel, spending time at the beach, and spending time with family and friends. One of her favorite pastimes is dog sitting for her many friends and families and donating dog beds to one of her favorite local charities in Delaware.

# Judy Cooper

Known for her daring spirit since childhood, Judy has gone on to experience adventures such as completing a solo parachute jump, hot air ballooning, taking a mule ride down the Grand Canyon, snorkeling through the second largest barrier reef in the world and zip lining over the jungle in Belize. Often filled with fear, she hasn't allowed it to interfere with the thrill of the adventure!

Equally bold in her passion for child advocacy, she single-handedly took on four different national governments while living overseas, in a successful quest to enrich her family through the adoption of a twenty-month-old infant from an orphanage in Romania. Soon afterwards, she was appointed by the Governor of Oregon as a Commissioner on the State Child Care Commission and became a trained volunteer child advocate with the non-profit CASA organization.

Born in Austria, Judy has lived in five different countries and traveled to eleven, with her favorite destinations being London, the Orkney Islands and Belize. Prior to starting her own real estate investment business in America, she progressed through both the domestic and international banking industries to become a "Money Desk" Manager, and a Trust Administrator in the offshore finance center of Guernsey (off the coast of France).

She currently resides in the beautiful Pacific Northwest and considers her greatest successes in life to be the relationship with her husband, Chris, the raising of three wonderful sons, and the adoption of her "little light."

# Steven Dotson, DC

Dr. Steven Dotson is proud to call Texas home and is the owner of Cornerstone Health and Wellness, a chiropractic clinic offering acute, corrective, and wellness care. Steve and his beautiful wife, Melanie have been married for twenty years. They have three amazing children: Payton, Ian, and Mia. Steve is an Army Veteran and served seven years as a Military Police officer.

The Army gave him the opportunity to work in other countries such as Germany, the Netherlands, Norway, Denmark, Turkey, Italy, Kuwait, and Iraq. At the request of his mother, he left the Army to help with the family business. Steve always had the desire to work in healthcare and decided to become a physical therapist. That direction changed while visiting family in Vietnam.

After a few days of being in the country, he contracted the flu. He felt as if he was on his death bed. He was treated by an uncle with acupuncture, cupping, Gua Sha, hydration, and adjustments. It was the spinal adjustments that made him feel instant relief and, in that moment, he found chiropractic care to be the vehicle to his life's purpose.

> "The doctor of the future will give no medicine, but will interest his patient in the care of the human frame, in diet, and in the cause and prevention of disease"
> —THOMAS EDISON

## *Kirsten Fagan*

Kirsten Fagan spent the first half of her life moving around, living in the Midwest and Hawaii. In 2004, she moved to Alabama and a few years later she met and married her sweetheart, Josh. Kirsten and her husband have two beautiful little girls. Kirsten is also a dog mom and a gardener. She has a deep love of music, and she loves to craft (when time allows).

Kirsten spent fifteen years working in healthcare, loving and caring for the elderly. It was during this time that she cultivated her uncanny gift for intuition and empathy. She knows what's needed in any given scenario to keep operations gently moving forward. Kirsten worked as Unit Coordinator for two Specialty Care Facilities where she quickly learned how to provide a wide range of support to wellness professionals, patients and their families.

In 2014, with an eight-month-old baby and the amazing support of her family, Kirsten graduated with a Bachelor's degree from the University of South Alabama.

In 2018, Kirsten made the decision to begin working from home and began building her business, B & G Virtual Solutions. She loves to learn new things, which has played a large part in her personal and professional growth. Kirsten thrives off of her decision to support Life Coaches, as they help others learn to live fulfilling and happy lives. More recently, Kirsten decided to lean into her love of travel and became a Travel Agent and expanded her already booming business.

## *Svetlana Farwell*

Svetlana Farwell was born and raised in the former Soviet Union, the part which is now the Russian Federation. She's been on both sides of the Iron Curtain, and personally lived through the most significant events of world history. This makes her teenage kids come to the conclusion that she's officially "a dinosaur." All five of them were born and raised in Texas but have not [yet] acquired a single pair of cowboy boots or a bolo tie.

Svetlana has traveled to most states within the US, but still has a few spots in the world on her wish list to visit someday. She also fully intends to go on a cruise at least once in her lifetime. She has two step cats and two grand guinea pigs, which she enjoys spoiling every now and then, before handing them right back to their rightful owners. While her parents were avid gardeners (they had to be, to make a living), Svetlana is still in search of the right shade of green for either one of her thumbs.

Svetlana lives in Hurst, TX with her best friend and partner of eight years and works in the corporate world of the US, the largest third-party hotel management company with over fifteen hundred hotels, resorts, and conference centers throughout North America and Caribbean and ninety-three internationally. She enjoys a good game of sudoku, fresh cut flowers, dark chocolate, and a good laugh with, or at the expense of, her closest friends.

## Scott Finkelstein

Scott Finkelstein was born in Queens, NY and raised in Plainview, Long Island. He is the youngest of three. He grew up in the printing industry, in his father's footsteps at Jaylor Printing in New York. While Scott made his journey to the Dallas area and stayed in printing for twenty-five years, he decided to make a career change and is currently President of "Next Door Painting," which entails interior and exterior painting for residential homes and commercial business.

While Scott does love his job, he is also a father to seven children. Scott has settled in Keller, Texas to raise his family and is currently living his best life. Scott loves travel, movies, family road trips, and his dogs River and Fiona. Scott is also a great friend and mentor and just an all-around genuine person.

# *Tiffany Martin Finkelstein*

Tiffany Martin Finkelstein, born and raised in Fort Worth, Texas, the youngest of eight children. She is also the mother of seven. Starting out on her journey in life she owned a little boutique in the Texas Christian University (TCU) area. Thereafter, she worked for Southwest Airlines where she was Activity Director for reservations. While raising children, she ran various businesses and currently owns a Hair Salon in Fort Worth.

Tiffany loves to travel, loves being with her husband and children, basically living her best life. Tiffany is kind, loving and excited about this new journey.

# Dawn L. Hargraves, Esq.

Dawn L. Hargraves was born and raised in Suffolk County, New York, where she continues to reside except for those three months each year that she resides in the Oceanside Village of Ocean Beach, where she holds the elected office of Trustee.

She is a practicing attorney whose work is focused on assisting men and women through the difficult process of divorce. Her professional work is rooted in addressing all aspects of the uncoupling process with compassion, support and integrity. She has many accomplishments in this area including NAPW Woman of the Year, Top Attorneys of North America and 10 Best Attorneys—American Institute of Family Law Attorneys.

When Dawn is not working, she is involved in and sits on several community organization boards raising money for those in need.

While Dawn is busy with her professional and volunteer life, she believes her most important role is that of "mom." She is most passionate about raising her two teenage daughters, Kate and Kimberly. She loves being the mom that doesn't say no to taking them on all sorts of adventures, including hang gliding, musical concerts and traveling to exotic beaches. She is grateful for the time she spends with her daughters and looks forward to continuing their travels throughout the United States and abroad.

# *Diana Cherryn Kelly, Ph.D.*

Co-Founder and Managing Partner of an educational consultancy and a social enterprise in the land of sand dunes, date palms and camels where today, instead of camels, Lamborghinis, Rolls Royce, Ashton Martins and Ferraris swarm the streets. Residing in Dubai, Dr. Diana Cherryn Kelly, is a Malaysian national of Indian descent.

She is a globetrotter, widely traveled from Asia to the Middle East and the Americas, advocating for social transformation through education. With her passion for public service, she gets involved from the grassroots level. Dr. Kelly is also on the board of directors of non-governmental organizations (NGO's) in Toronto, Canada and Kenya in Africa.

Dedicating her life at a young age, Dr. Kelly's vision and mission of building a brighter future for our children, youth and women drives her. Her work has touched and changed lives. It has also inspired and encouraged the hearts of those who work alongside her, the ones who have given of themselves, their resources, time, and expertise.

Over the last several years, in partnership with government entities, corporate leaders and professionals, her work has reached into the lands of the Middle East and the Arabic Gulf countries with transformational educational programs such as STEM Education, Financial Literacy, Career Development and Early Childhood Development.

Dr. Kelly is also a proud mother of four children. Young at heart and spirit, she has a zest for life, love and laughter. Her favorite hobbies are reading, walking in nature, swimming, yoga and simply enjoying time with family and friends.

## *Hannah Kersey*

Hannah Kersey, a Dallas, Texas resident works as a bartender at "FNG Eats." She studied Theatre at Dallas Tech for three years. She aspires to work for a national park and lean into living the life she would love to live.

Hannah's family is an important part of her life. She enjoys spending time with her brothers, Philip, Walker and Hunter. When she is not busy working, she is going on adventures. She loves to camp, hike and go on annual road trips with her dad, Russell. She loves to spend time with her mom, Laura, and enjoys going to the arcade and trying new restaurants with her friends. Hannah has a little fur baby named Jupiter. Jupiter is a rescue cat she found while at college.

# *Philip Kersey*

Philip Kersey, a Fort Worth Texas native is a fun-loving, caring, food connoisseur. He has worked as a CNA caring for Alzheimer's patients, driven eighteen wheelers for Swift Transportation through forty-eight different states, and he is currently the team lead for twenty-nine apartment complexes for a trash valet service.

Philip is currently in school learning to be a software developer. He dreams of opening his own business and traveling the world, while serving others from the comforts of his own laptop. In his spare time, he loves to try new foods, meet new people and travel. He loves to sing, read, cook, play tabletop board games with his family and play video games.

Philip is a man of many talents and he loves to learn new things and try new things. His goal is to live life to the fullest.

## *Ellen Moseley-May*

Ellen Moseley-May is an author, speaker, coach and artist residing in Livingston, Texas. She is the author of "Surviving a Murder" a story of forgiveness. Most days you can find her sitting outside her studio on her deck with her brush in hand and her pup curled up at her feet because, let's face it, creating art is always better with dogs. Ellen is mostly known for being a beach obsessed gypsy soul with a love for crazy clothes loaded with color, art, Jesus and gymnastics.

People often refer to her as the girl who jumps in with two feet and never thinks about whether she will be able to swim. She built her first business, "Moseley Gymnastics," thirty-three years ago with the $350 she received in gifts for high school graduation and a fearless desire to change lives. Many people will tell you she is extremely opinionated, but also incredibly driven, inspiring and motivating. She loves serving the world by encouraging others to grow personally, spiritually and professionally without sacrificing their authenticity or integrity. You could say, she's a cheerleader to the world.

The things she is most passionate about in life are: Jesus, who drives her every dream and vision, her family and making memories with them that will last longer than her life here on earth. Art, because she not only loves to create it, but she loves sharing with others how they, too, can tap into their own creative spirit. YES, she believes we all have one. She loves to build up and encourage people to believe in themselves and the dreams they have. Ellen also has a deep passion for exercise and nutrition because of her belief that self-care and self-love are key to living a happy and balanced life.

When she is not busy painting or creating custom handmade gifts in her studio, you can find her teaching life skills to her students through the sport of gymnastics. As a coach of thirty-five years, she has been named Coach of the Year and honored as an Outstanding Graduate of her former high school for her contributions to her community. That notwithstanding, as often as possible, you can find her traveling with her hubby in their motorhome to as many beaches as possible and collecting sea shells and sea glass to use in many of her art creations, or teaching her grandson, Jackson, the joys of art and Jesus and how to worship with the gifts we are given.

Ellen's greatest desire is to leave a feeling of belief in everyone she meets and to be able to spark in them a desire to follow their dreams and live whatever life makes them shine the brightest. She believes if she can do that, then she's fulfilled her purpose.

## *April Mazzoni*

April Mazzoni, born and raised in Maryland, until the ripe ol' age of ten . . . Now considers herself, after twenty-six years, a native of Colorado, where she lives with her son and two daughters.

In her early twenties', starting her career in dental, she spent over twelve years in the dental field. She moved into orthodontic care because she loved seeing how happy a child was when she took their braces off and he or she loved their beautiful new smile. During that time, April knew she wanted to help people on a deeper, more emotional level and spend more time with her three beautiful children.

She then decided to work on her business from home, being a photographer for those who have been abused and scarred in some way. With similar life experiences, a beautiful soul and such a deep love for others, she uses her love of music and photos to show them that they AREN'T broken or alone and that their voices CAN be heard. She uses her skills to give them the confidence to KNOW and FEEL that they are beautiful.

When April isn't busy being a full-time mom, she focuses on her profound love of music, taking weekly guitar lessons and enjoying live music with her friends. Fond memories of her childhood have her and her family vacationing at one of her favorite places, Ocean City, MD.

# Todd Miller

Todd Miller was born and raised in the beautiful state of Kentucky, just outside of the Louisville metropolitan area, in Oldham County. Home of horses, bourbon, bluegrass and great food. He now resides in Tucson Arizona, home to the unique flora and fauna of the Sonoran Desert.

Todd was raised in a Christian home with four younger siblings. Despite growing up in a beautiful country setting, Todd suffered several traumas early in life, including bullying at school, that would lead to lengthy bouts of severe depression and anxiety throughout his early life. Though always well liked, Todd suffered self-doubt and struggled with money issues for decades. He was open to his spirituality at an early age, but just didn't know how to harness the power we all hold within.

With strong will, tenacity and facing all adversities head on, he moved into the world of healthcare and nursing, working in the fields of emergency, cardiac care, psychiatric and pediatric care. Being the eldest of five children gave him a strong sense of looking out for others and responsibility. Todd has worked with many healing modalities throughout the years seeking to heal himself and others along the way. Todd is a Certified Reiki Master and ordained as a minister of the Universal Life Church in Mesto, California. So, if you need a last-minute shotgun wedding, hit him up. He is passionate about humor (yes, he can say off the wall stuff that can make you pee your pants) photography, nature, learning and teaching others how to use food to heal the body.

He is an amazing home chef that cooks with organic and whole food recipes. Todd is altruistic by nature and now older and, hopefully, wiser is learning how important it is to live in the NOW, not in the past. He integrates forgiveness, love, abundance, gratitude, prayer and meditation into his daily practice.

Though distance separates him from his family, he loves them dearly and travels to see them as often as he can. He is the proud father to his artistically talented son, Joshua, an amazing daughter in-law and two beautiful grandchildren. Looking back, Todd is amazed to have witnessed the love, forgiveness and perseverance that binds him to his family to this day.

Decades after "thinking about it" Todd is NOW the proud owner of his real estate company, "HS Property Solutions LLC," where he continues to help others in distressed situations, assisting individuals and families transition to a fresh new start in life.

# Cynthia Morales

Cynthia Morales grew up in New York City but found her way to Florida in her young adult years, to build a legacy for her family.

After having a successful career in the banking industry, Cynthia decided it was time to spread her entrepreneurial wings and lean into her passion for jewelry and clothing. She started her own businesses, "CMor Jewelry" and "CynFully Exquisite Closet Sale." Both businesses were founded and built with the mindfulness of serving others in their journey to becoming successful entrepreneurs. Cynthia inspires, coaches, and trains her teams to be all they can be personally and professionally.

When not building a legacy in her businesses, Cynthia loves spending time with her daughter Ariana and her precious grandson, Zaire.

Cynthia recently purchased her dream home, "The Lake House" as she affectionately refers to it, and she embraces the dream that God has given her. She is grateful for the beautiful homestead He provided for her family to share and enjoy to the fullest.

Cynthia's passion and zeal for life is contagious! She loves traveling, coaching others into success, being present for her mommy, daughter, and grandson. She's passionate in her pursuit of living into her authentic self and is a true friend to all that have the honor of knowing her.

# Nikki George Papadakis

Nikki George Papadakis, "Though she be but little, she is fierce!" She radiates positive energy that lights up any room she walks into. Her mindset and outlook on life has given her the ability to motivate others to achieve their highest potential by re-patterning their thinking so that they too, can live their best lives.

With over fifteen years of experience working in various industries focused on customer service, she has mastered skills in communication, understanding and awareness. She is a great listener and is truly interested in what others have to say and how they think. She feels most grateful when she sees shifts in other people's lives when they have taken her advice and applied it.

She always says, "When you wake up every morning, you have two choices. You can choose to be positive or you can choose to be negative. The choice is yours. *Change your thinking, change your life!*"

## Shannon Pattillo

Shannon Pattillo grew up in the Bay Area of San Francisco but spent her summers on her grandparents farm, riding horses, mowing lawns, catching fireflies and going to many St Louis Cardinals' games.

She considers herself both country and city. She grew up in the best of both worlds. She is a constant work in progress and enjoys visiting wineries, cooking, painting, traveling, and a good fire on a rainy day.

She is a proud mom, loves her friends and family and is excited to see what life has in store for her.

# Jamie Salerno

Jamie Salerno is a twenty-year veteran of the financial industry with an MBA and a BS in Marketing. Jamie has been working her way through all facets of the financial industry while cultivating her love for writing. She has owned her own mortgage processing company, been a licensed mortgage broker, a district manager, and is currently a Financial Center Leader of a financial institution. She loves helping people reach their financial dreams and strives to make those around her feel loved and supported.

Having been in eight schools by the sixth grade, Jamie knows no strangers. Her love for travel runs deep and remains a passion of hers to this day. She has one fur-baby, a beautiful miniature poodle named King Kong aka KiKo, and a tight knit group of family and friends. Jamie is currently on a self-awareness mission to improve what she takes in and puts out into the universe. When she is not working, she loves the beach, riding her bike, reading, spending time with family and friends and playing with KiKo.

## Jackie Scott

Jackie is your average blue-collar worker with a not-so-average passion for life, personal development, and spiritual healing. She was born in Coeur d' Alene, Idaho where she visits yearly. She grew up in central Pennsylvania, where she currently resides with her husband and family.

Growing up in Sunbury, Jackie discovered her passion and drive for personal development. Just after high school she joined the United States Navy and served on the USS Arleigh Burke for four years. It was in her mid-twenties, when she finally cultivated and began sharing her passions through her work at Flagger Force Traffic Control by training, coaching, and helping others achieve their goals. Jackie expanded her vision and is the founder of Mystic Elevations where she focuses on empowering individuals to take charge of their lives through energy healing treatments.

When she is not working, she enjoys spending time with family at gatherings, watching science fiction and romantic comedies, traveling to new places and enjoying the journey of each life adventure.

# Jack Smith Jr.

Like any serial entrepreneur, Jack Smith Jr is responsible for a lot of things . . . probably too many to count.

He is a successful entrepreneur (that includes a Janitorial cleaning company, a frozen yogurt shop and an online business), who is also the Chairman of his non-profit organization, "The Art Of Charity." In 2020, he formed this non-profit to help people that were going through a hard time due to COVID-19, while he was struggling to keep his own head above water. He feels that his calling from God is to help the less fortunate. Along with volunteering his time with the Greater Pittsburgh Community Food Bank, he has found time to study Global Sports Management with New York University. He is a self-proclaimed Fantasy Sports guru who loves to play daily.

He is also a Pittsburgh sports fan but does not like the Steelers (yes, I said it). Jack lives in Pittsburgh, Pennsylvania with his three daughters, Tesia, Zaynah, Iyonna and a crazy cat who likes to open doors and thinks he is a watch dog!

Keep in touch with Jack via the web:

Website: www.theartofcharity.com
Facebook: http://www.facebook.com/jacksmith
Instagram: https://instagram.com/finallyhere1

## *Linda Walker*

Linda Walker, a native Texan, has lived across the beautiful state throughout her eighty years of life. The daughter of a Methodist minister, she moved frequently and that afforded her the ability to have new experiences and adventures growing up.

Raised in the First United Methodist Church (FUMC) and serving as a lay leader for decades, Linda enjoyed being involved in the many ministries and activities of the church. She especially loved ringing handbells and singing in the choir. Linda tirelessly served in the Livingston, TX FUMC church program, Life 101 for several years making sure numerous people received a lovely meal after their studies.

Linda currently resides in Plano, TX and works part time at J Jill clothiers in Willowbend mall where she thrives in socializing with co-workers and meeting new people while serving them in their clothing needs.

Linda is the mother of four amazing adult daughters, and she passed on her love of travel, music, faith, and parenting to each of them. Linda also has eleven beautiful grandchildren whom she loves dearly.

During her down time, Linda enjoys keeping a beautiful yard, a good movie, dining out, spending time with family and reading about local and world history and culture.

# *Janette Wold*

Janette Wold is an inspirational and spiritual life coach and is Founder and Owner of "Self-Possessed Coaching LLC" Janette helps her clients find and build their confidence, gain hope and clarity and keep themselves soul centered. Her passion is to help her clients release themselves from traumas that they have experienced and live the happier, healthier, and free life that they have always dreamt of.

For over thirty years, Janette has researched and implemented many tools to overcome childhood trauma and subjection to narcissism in her own life. She has studied behavior patterning and behavior changes to eradicate the cycle these negative experiences can replicate. She believes that what has happened to us does not define who we can become and only gives us the feedback we need to become stronger, more self-possessed souls.

Her love for life is contagious and her best days are spent with family traveling, learning, exploring, teaching, and loving!

## *About the Author*

Inspiring and empowering those who are drawn to her, LAURA K WALKER coaches her clients to live their highest vision in the context of love, joy, core values, and Divine inspiration. Her passion is teaching clients to unlock their true God-given potential, achieve outrageous success and live a life they love Living!

For over twenty-five years, Laura has continually studied and implemented transformational success principles in her own life, in her workshops, and coaching programs helping people break through self-limiting blocks and human paradigms, so they can proactively achieve greater results than they have ever known before, personally and professionally.

When Laura is not coaching and mentoring people into patterns of success, she enjoys spending time with her fiancé Hanson, her four grown children Philip, Hunter, Hannah, Walker, and her bonus son, Joshua.

She loves dining out, sharing wine with gal pals, and traveling the world with friends and family. If there is live music, you will probably see Laura there. If you ask her about her perception of life, she's certainly living a life she absolutely loves loving and loves to teach people how to do the same.

Made in the USA
Middletown, DE
11 October 2022